THE WILD WEST
ON 5 BITS A DAY

D0089791

JOAN TAPPER

THE WILD WEST

ON 5 BITS A DAY

★ ★ ★ ★ ★

with 97 illustrations, 5 in color

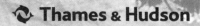

Thames & Hudson

 CONTENTS ★

PRECEDING PAGES
Chestnut Street, Leadville,
Colorado.

★ BEFORE YOU GO ★

IMAGINING THE WEST

Vast prairies, towering mountains, powerful rivers cascading through tortuous canyons; gold prospectors, Indians, and trail-riding cowboys. Who today, in 1880, has not been tantalized by hints of what lies beyond the Mississippi? From reports of intrepid explorers, frontiersmen, and surveyors to stories from adventurous fortune seekers and emigrants, we've been swept away by visions of a heroic landscape peopled with characters larger than life. And if some of these portraits are painted with the brush of fiction, well, that only heightens our enjoyment of the tales – and perhaps our curiosity to see the West for ourselves.

Take *Buffalo Bill: King of the Border Men.* Ned Buntline's dime novel may be full of imaginary acts of derring-do, but his real-life hero, William Cody, has been both an army scout and a buffalo hunter. And what about *Roughing It*? Leave it to Mark Twain to stretch the truth as far as his celebrated Calaveras County frog could jump, but there's no doubt he's met his share of characters in the Comstock, California, and beyond.

ABOVE Isabella Bird dressed for adventure in *A Lady's Life in the Rocky Mountains.*

OPPOSITE A cowboy on a cattle drive can spend months in the saddle.

" These stormy American sunsets are startling, barbaric, even savage in their brilliancy of tone, in their profusion of colour, in their great streaks of red and broad flashes of yellow fire; startling, but never repulsive to the senses or painful to the eye. "

The Earl of Dunraven, *The Great Divide*, 1876

So many travelers have astounded us with the obstacles they faced. Writers like trader Josiah Gregg, who braved the perils of the Santa Fe Trail, and Isabella Bird, who set her sights on Colorado's Rocky Mountains. *Harper's*, the *Atlantic*, *Scribner's*, and *Frank Leslie's Illustrated Newspaper* have all filled their pages with reports from frontier outposts, not only with the words of their traveling correspondents, but with images as well. Who does not marvel at Thomas Moran's sketches and paintings of Yellowstone, or William Henry Jackson's panoramic photographs of natural wonders and new towns? Carleton Watkins's images of Yosemite can be viewed in your own

ABOVE Albert Bierstadt's *Yosemite Valley*, painted in 1868, depicts the magnificence of the California wilderness on a large scale and in vivid color. Looking down the valley, Sentinel Rock and Cathedral Rocks on the left face El Capitan on the right.

stereoscope, while Albert Bierstadt's enormous canvases of mountains and chasms are dazzling beyond belief.

These stories and pictures will convince you that the sights of Europe have met their match in the grandeur of America's wilderness. Forego the musty churches of the Old World for majestic cathedrals of rock. Bypass the museums of ancient civilizations for the excitement of new cultures. The West is wild indeed, with sights, sounds, people, and experiences that will expand your horizons wide as the prairie sky itself.

OPPOSITE On track for success, transcontinental routes tout the comforts of their sleeping cars as well as their new service, speed, and even steamship connections around the globe.

WHY GO NOW?

There is no better time than now to explore the West. For two decades a transcontinental railroad has tied the cities of the Atlantic to the Pacific, and now more than one cross-country route beckons, with branch lines that will take you into the burgeoning towns. Prices are easily within your reach, although it must be admitted that five bits probably won't sustain you for a day anymore. A half-eagle, as a $5 gold piece is known, will more than suffice, however. If you have a spark of adventure in you – man and woman alike! – the West awaits.

But don't delay. The very trains that will make your journey easier than Mark Twain's twenty years ago are carrying the settlers who will inevitably tame the American frontier. Emigrants are turning the unbroken prairie into fields of wheat. Ranchers are beginning to gather their open-range herds of cattle behind an invention called "barbwire." This could be your last chance to see the West while it's still wild, and meet people as fascinating and exotic as any you'll find abroad.

Mormons, for example, have created their own society in Deseret, as they call Utah Territory. They are a people of amazing contradictions: Women have the right to vote in local elections but they are subject to the rites of polygamy, the custom of plural marriage. Their former leader Brigham Young – who was said to be sealed in marriage to more than fifty women – recently passed away, but the power of the Mormon Church

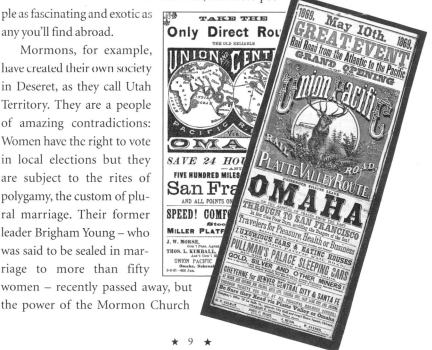

continues, and Salt Lake City thrives as a not-to-be-missed stop on any Western journey.

The new mining towns of the West are veritable Babels, as immigrants from Europe have flocked there to seek the earth's mineral riches. Anyone with curiosity about inventions and technology should meet the miners and engineers who are moving mountains and building railroads over daunting peaks to carry ore to market. (Would-be investors might also take note.)

Meanwhile the forts of the West continue to offer hospitality, as they did to overland settlers for many years. A visit will introduce you to cavalry officers and their wives who will be eager for any news you bring. In return you'll hear firsthand of army exploits in recent Indian wars.

You needn't fear the Indians – unless you venture to the wilds of Arizona Territory, where Geronimo and his Apaches still pose dangers to the casual tourist. Elsewhere most tribes have moved to reservations, usually in controversial circumstances. Several eloquent Indian leaders have begun to speak at meeting halls, where you may hear them discuss their plight and the disappearing ways of their people.

Are you curious about cowboys – the horsemen who push thousands of cattle on months-long journeys from Texas to outposts like Dodge City, Kansas? If you meet them in town, you may find them a bit rambunctious. But buy the buckaroos a drink, and perhaps they'll regale you with tales of days in the saddle and nights spent sleeping under the stars.

SAMPLE COSTS

Fare by railroad from Chicago to San Francisco	$118
Return [from San Francisco to Chicago]	$118
To Salt Lake and return	$6
To the Big Trees, Yosemite, and return	$38

For sleeping cars, about $3 per day

Add for hotel accommodations, $3.50 per day; for horses and guides on the Yosemite, $5 per day; for meals on the railroad, $2 per day. To see Lake Tahoe, Donner Lake, and Virginia City will cost you $20 more.

Charles Nordhoff, *California, How to Go There*, 1872

" ...Before this terrible railroad is omnipresent – before saddles and walking-boots become things of the past – ride and tramp! For that is the way to see that best part of the world which nature still claims for her own.**"**

John Codman, *The Mormon Country.*
A Summer with the Latter Day Saints, 1874

Horse-drawn wagon or iron horse? *Frank Leslie's Illustrated Newspaper* makes clear that there are now two ways of heading west.

Frontier watering holes are the place to meet the gamblers, adventurers, and ladies of uncertain reputation you've heard stories about, but be fore-warned before you try your luck with them at cards or games of chance. Many of these colorful customers make a living from preying on unsuspecting travelers, and even honest Westerners are fond of playing pranks on dudes. But don't let that deter you from visiting the saloon: It's just as likely to be the social center of the community as the local church – if there is one.

Wherever you go, and whomever you meet, you'll find that Westerners have an enterprising resilience and a lively way of looking at the world. You might find it so intriguing that you'll be tempted to join them for good.

★ 2 ★

GETTING THERE

THE TRANSCONTINENTAL JOURNEY

Ever since the golden spike was struck in the final rail in 1869, it's been possible to cross the continent with increasing facility. Put aside what you've heard about train-robbing desperadoes, Indian raids, catastrophic derailments, and storms of alkali and dust. Today, reaching San Francisco from

BELOW It was toasts and handshakes all round on May 10, 1869, as locomotives from the Central Pacific and the Union Pacific railroads met at Promontory Summit, Utah.

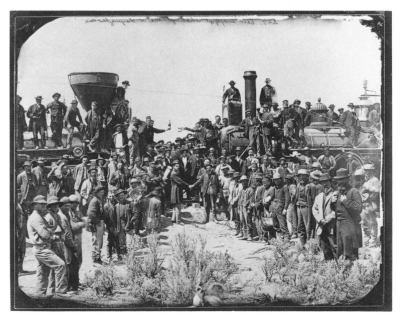

ABOVE Not everyone can afford a Pullman car. Ordinary passengers do the best they can, as they settle in for the night on a transcontinental journey.

the East is a commonplace journey – or would be if there weren't so many marvels en route. If you simply want to rush across the continent, you can make your way by rail to Omaha, Nebraska, board the Union Pacific and ride to Ogden, Utah, then change for the Central Pacific, which will deposit you in Vallejo, California, where you take the ferry for San Francisco. Omaha to the coast in five days – amazing!

Thanks to the inventive and entrepreneurial spirit of George Pullman, you can, if you wish, tuck in each night between fresh sheets on berths that fold by day into discreet shelves or transform into easy chairs and sofas. Those who would like to travel like a king – or as the Russian Grand Duke Alexis did a decade ago – can order up the ultimate in luxury: a suite of three Pullman cars that included a parlor car, a dining car, and a sleeping car. Even the most demanding traveler, however, would be pleased with the privacy and appointments of a hotel car, which resembles a comfortable living room at home, with pillowy sofas and writing tables, and comes with its own

" The old assertion that man is at bottom a savage animal finds confirmation strong in a sleeping-car. "

Frank Leslie, *Across the Continent*, 1878

kitchen with 20-gallon tanks for running water, as well as a wine closet, a china closet, a linen closet, and a pantry big enough to stock food for thirty people. It's perfect if you want to bring along your Odd Fellows lodge, your literary society, or your hunting and fishing friends – or have a family as big as Brigham Young's.

The majority of wayfarers, though, will travel alone or in twos and threes in sleeping cars, divided into rather cozy berths or slightly more spacious drawing rooms. For adventurers whose desire to see the West exceeds their need for comfort – or available hard currency – there is the ordinary passenger car and sometimes an even more bare-bones emigrant car. The seats may leave you stiff and aching after several days crossing plains and mountains, but they'll get you to your destination nonetheless.

There are dining cars – moving restaurants, really – on the rail lines up to Omaha, and someday they may be added on the routes farther west. Imagine sitting at your table, watching the endless grasslands of Kansas or the Dakota Territory roll beyond your window as you enjoy a dinner of breaded veal cutlets, with a glass of claret. Until then, passengers will continue to disembark for meals three times a day at stations along the route. At the best-run stations there may be hot soup, broiled trout, and fresh vegetables served on white tablecloths by cordial waiters; at other stops the dishes might be laid out on rumpled red cloths and restricted to boiled beef, roast beef, salt beef, and bacon. But you won't go hungry.

Sometimes there's time for a leisurely dinner. The Ogden Eating House advertises the fact that all trains stop in the town for one to two hours – plenty of time to get a "first class meal" for "$1 in Coin, $1.25 in Currency." For other places, like Elko, Nevada, where the stop lasts only twenty-five minutes, passengers can have the porter telegraph ahead and order meals of game, trout, or chicken dinner at a cost of just 75 cents in coin, or $1 in currency. A young man named Fred Harvey, who operates the lunch counter at the train station in Topeka, Kansas, now has a contract to open other restau-

Gateway to a new life: Characters galore toting all kinds of baggage crowd the emigrant waiting room of the Union Pacific depot in Omaha, Nebraska.

rants on the Atchison, Topeka & Santa Fe line that will accommodate the railroad schedules. For now a prudent traveler should probably pack a picnic basket, just in case the train is delayed beyond the scheduled mealtime, the press of the crowd doesn't allow you to be seated in time, or snow on the tracks holds you up for a day or two. Better to be prepared for such adventures. (Remember the Donner Party…?) If you go through your stores, or just want to savor some fresh, local tidbits, you may be able to purchase snacks from vendors who come onto the cars. At stations near farms women and girls might offer baked prairie chickens; near orchards farther west, there might be fruit or jugs of cider for refreshment.

Even if you decide to speed across the continent without side trips, you'll be able to see a bit of untamed wilderness from your railway car, though

" Now, it wasn't wholly an uneventful trip through the buffalo grassland; we certainly had some excitement. While in Nebraska, we passed by a recent train wreck. "

Mrs. Frank Leslie, *California: A Pleasure Trip From Gotham to the Golden Gate*, 1877

after just a single decade of transcontinental railways, some sights have already begun to disappear. Where herds of buffalo once thundered past, inviting marksmen to shoot the animals through the windows, few traces of this majestic symbol of the West are still visible. Instead there are piles of buffalo bones at certain stations along the route, and you may observe your fellow passengers carrying valises of buffalo hide.

On the plains you'll undoubtedly spot prairie dogs, antelope, and bounding jackrabbits. (There also have been reports of a creature called a jackalope – perhaps you'll be the first to see one!) You may catch a glimpse of

ABOVE Buffalo once were so plentiful on the plains that train passengers barely had to leave their seats to shoot them. Hunters have drastically reduced the animals' numbers.

OPPOSITE The Deadwood stagecoach, "Old Silver Top," has been a frequent target of robbers. No wonder the driver has a shotgun on his lap.

ALL THE WORLD RIDES A STAGE

Wooden Concord coaches have transported travelers throughout the West for decades. The original 1827 design was the work of the Abbot Downing Company of Concord, New Hampshire. Drawn by six horses, each coach usually seats nine passengers inside, with an extra seat by the driver. There are also windows and doors, two glass lights, and a huge trunk for baggage. The vehicles are known for their swaying motion, the result of leather braces that cradle the carriage body like an egg. That hasn't dissuaded passengers on the roughest routes from complaining that they arrive at their destinations somewhat scrambled.

Despite their large size, when Concord coaches are full, it's a crowded ride, so rules of etiquette have developed, as reported in the 1877 *Omaha Herald*:

• Don't smoke a strong pipe inside, especially early in the morning. Spit on the leeward side of the coach. If you have anything to take in a bottle, pass it around; a man who drinks by himself in such a case is lost to all human feeling.

• Don't swear, nor lop over on your neighbor when sleeping. Don't ask how far it is to the next station until you get there.

• Don't discuss politics or religion, nor point out places on the road where horrible murders have been committed.

• Don't imagine for a moment you are going on a picnic; expect annoyance, discomfort and some hardships. If you are disappointed, thank heaven.

curious dwellings that resemble dugouts topped by sod; these are the homes erected by immigrants laying claim to a farm. As you travel westward, snow-capped mountains will herald your arrival near Cheyenne. Later, brooding canyons lead the way into Ogden. If you continue straight to California, there is the exhilarating conquest of the summit of the Sierras before you drop down into flatland again.

If you accomplish only that much, you'll still bring back tales to regale your friends for weeks. But to claim the title of true traveler, you must break the cross-country trip and set off for the hinterlands. You will probably have to forego the Pullman cars and strike out in overland or mail stages to reach some of the West's newest and most exciting towns. If you have a literary bent, remember that Mark Twain turned the discomforts of his journey into a bestseller. And what's a little jolting and close quarters compared to the adventures, sights, and characters that await you!

CHOOSING AN ITINERARY

Horace Greeley may have said "Go West," but when actually planning a trip, you'll need to be more specific. Unless you have a year or two at leisure (and perhaps an unlimited supply of golden double eagles) you will have to choose the places that most intrigue you.

How intrepid do you feel? Do you want the comforts and conveniences that come with a railway depot or are you willing to spend a few hours or a day on a Concord stagecoach or even in a saddle?

You could ride narrow-gauge railway lines around mountain slopes to the mining towns of Colorado – Leadville, for example – or detour to sample the hospitality of Fort Laramie, which is now a departure point for gold prospectors heading for the Black Hills and Deadwood. Transfer to the Utah Central Railroad at Ogden to see Salt Lake City and perhaps hazard a dip in the Great Salt Lake. At Reno you can also venture onto the Virginia & Truckee for a stop at Virginia City, where the riches of the Comstock Lode have given birth to a metropolis that rivals San Francisco. If you take the

In his *Scenes of Wonder and Curiosity in California*, James Hutchings lures travelers with an engraving of Yosemite Falls' triple cascade.

Atchison, Topeka & Santa Fe line from Topeka, you can gauge for yourself the truth of what you've read of cowboy towns like Dodge City. For Fort Worth, you'll need a trip on the Texas & Pacific or the Missouri–Kansas–Texas lines. You can even connect to Santa Fe itself, where the ghosts of Old Spain imbue the *villa* with an atmosphere like no other. If you hanker to see Arizona's Tombstone, though, be ready to climb aboard a stagecoach.

To experience the exhilaration of nature, you can travel to California and board a coach for a trip to the Big Trees and waterfalls of Yosemite. But if you truly long to leave the constraints of civilization behind, mount a horse and aim for the geysers and canyons of Yellowstone. You will be among the early visitors of our first national park, though surely not the last.

" There was no trail at all; only piles of stones here and there to mark the best route. But when at last we arrived we were amply repaid for our labor. Imagine a sheer cliff, sixteen hundred feet high… the water seems to fall out of the very sky itself… *"*

Joseph LeConte, *A Journal of Ramblings through the High Sierra of California by the University Excursion Party*, 1875

★ 19 ★

3

PRACTICAL ADVICE

WHERE TO STAY

In the West's biggest towns, don't be surprised to find two- and three-story hotels with all the latest conveniences: hot and cold water, gas lighting, excellent dining rooms, barber shops and billiard parlors for the gentlemen, and sitting rooms for the ladies. One fine hotel in Virginia City even has an elevator. In most locations you'll also have a choice of more modest boarding houses, with simple but comfortable rooms, and meals included. Of course, if you journey to the parks or land in a town that has sprung up only yesterday, you'll probably experience all the inconveniences that met earlier travelers: unfinished buildings with bedrooms divided only by cloth partitions; haphazard service or none at all. If accommodations are really scarce you may end up sharing space with a stranger. For these destinations it is best to keep your hopes high but your expectations low.

To explore the parks, why not hire an outfitter? (There are several advertised in the guidebooks issued by the transcontinental railways.) The company

will provide a guide, a cook, horses, and tents: everything you need to feel at one with nature.

A newly available tourist option is lodging on a working ranch, such as the one the Eaton brothers run near Medora, in Dakota Territory. Friends who came to visit enjoyed their Western hospitality so much that they stayed on and insisted on paying for the room and board. As a result, the Eatons are now inviting other "dudes" to come and experience the true West.

WHAT TO EAT

Railway or stagecoach station meals may tax your patience, as one traveler noted: "You find yourself having dinner at 7 A.M., supping at noon, and breakfasting somewhere about sundown, or in the middle of the night. As all the repasts are much the same, consisting of beefsteaks, pork, potatoes, hot biscuit…and coffee, this dislocation of meals does not so very much signify." But once you arrive in town, you may be amazed at the variety of culinary choices. Elaborate pastries, pies, and puddings will satisfy any sweet tooth, while ice cream parlors are pleasant destinations on hot afternoons. Tinned oysters in remote towns seem to cause the most astonish-

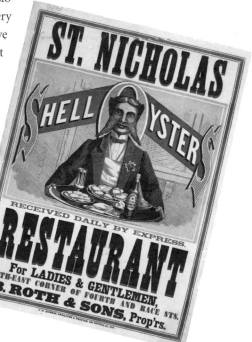

RIGHT No gourmet backwater, one Western restaurant promises delicacies on the half shell.

OPPOSITE The Walker House hotel advertises all its latest amenities in a railway guide.

ment, but, in fact, many chefs throughout the region seem determined to outdo New York's Delmonico restaurant. Colorado mining towns like Georgetown and Leadville excel in this regard, and Virginia City, too, prides itself on its fine tables; perhaps the prevalence of gold dust or silver nuggets has something to do with it.

In towns that thrive on the cattle business, you can order up tasty steaks and chops, and pork in all its variations is generally plentiful. On the cattle trail itself, daily menus revolve around salt pork, an occasional steak, beans, sourdough biscuits, and coffee, but a clever cook might vary the menu by preparing any game, fish, or turtles the cowboys catch. Some even soak sliced potatoes in saltwater and add vinegar to make a substitute for cucumbers.

You'll find the most unusual meals in the Southwestern territories, where Spanish and Indian traditions have seeped into the kitchen. Corn-meal tortillas – a kind of flat pancake – are a staple there, used to scoop up accompanying dishes like *frijoles* (beans). The flavors may be stronger than you're used to, thanks to the chili peppers that add spark. Just be sure when you reach for a glass of liquid that it's water, not whiskey, which packs a Western wallop of its own.

FOOD FIT FOR AN EX-PRESIDENT

When former President Ulysses S. Grant recently visited Leadville, the town pulled out all the stops, the festivities culminating with a grand banquet to prove that the town was no culinary backwater. The bill of fare for the occasion was printed in red on gold satin and is faithfully reproduced here:

BANQUET TO GENERAL U. S. GRANT
By the Citizens of Leadville, July 24, 1880

MENU

SOUPS
Puree of Califlower, a la Reine
Consomme Sevigne

HORS D'OEUVRE
Tomatoes · Cucumbers · Sardines
Olives

FISH
Speckled Trout Fried, au Beurre Frais
Potatoes Croquettes

ENTREES
Tenderloin of Beef, pique, a la Russe
Stuffed Tomatoes · Browned Potatoes
Cutlets of Spring Chicken, a la Perigeux
Sweet Breads en Caisse, a la Toulouse
Green Peas · Cauliflower
Young Duck, Farcie, Apple Sauce
Wild Pigeon, braise, au Riz
Mayonnaise of Shrimps
Chicken, en Bellevue

GROSSE PIECES
Galantine de Dinde, a la Parisienne
Jambon Socle, a la Regence
Salade de Legumes, a l'Italienne
Fontaine en Sucre File
Fancy Pyramid of Cakes

SUCRES
Egg Souffles, a la Vanille
Fruit Tarts
Meringues a la Geles
Neapolitan Ice Cream
Petti Fours · Fruits · Nuts
Coffee · Tea

CHUCKWAGON DELICACIES

One way to preserve the meat of a butchered steer on the trail is to make jerky, for which strips of beef are smoked over a fire. It can be fried in tallow before serving.

Prairie or mountain oysters – the fried testicles of a castrated bull – are a famous chuckwagon delicacy.

Marrow gut, another particular favorite, is made from the fresh, unwashed entrails of a cow, cut in 4-inch pieces and flavored with sage, salt, and pepper.

Then you have the recipe for "sonofabitch stew," which calls for 2 pounds of lean beef, half a calf heart, 1½ pounds of calf liver, 1 set of sweetbreads, 1 set of brains, 1 set of marrow gut, salt, pepper, and Louisiana hot sauce. Delicious.

OPPOSITE Cowboys on the trail in Kansas make quick work of an open-air supper. Shelves and compartments have turned the cattle-drive chuckwagon into a kitchen on wheels.

WHAT TO WEAR

Contrary to what you might expect, styles in the West don't lag far behind those of Eastern cities, thanks to magazines that keep even small-town dressmakers and milliners up to date. You'll undoubtedly want to pack a formal suit or dress – perhaps silk or cashmere – for elegant social gatherings or nights at the theater, especially if your itinerary takes you to Virginia City or San Francisco.

But don't neglect sturdy outfits for the journey itself, preferably in dark colors that will stand up to hard wear: a flannel shirt and buckskin (or even denim) trousers for the men; calico or durable muslin dresses for women. Isabella Bird discovered that after three months of travel in the Rocky Mountains, her wardrobe had been reduced to a single threadbare and much-darned change of clothes, "by legitimate wear, the depredations of calves, and the necessity of tearing some of them up for dish-cloths." Extra collars, cuffs, and pocket handkerchiefs should be tucked into the corners of your valise. And both men and women will want a warm coat, a hat with a brim – ladies can add veils – buckskin gloves, and thick boots.

Special clothing items have been developed to combat the extremes of the Western climate. British travel writer Richard Burton concocted an all-purpose garment for himself when he crossed the country some years ago: an "India-rubber blanket, pierced in the centre for a poncho, and garnished along the longer side with buttons, and corresponding elastic loops with a strap at the short end, converting it into a carpet bag – a 'sine qua non' from the equator to the pole." At the very least, take a duster (a full-length waterproof overcoat, slit up the back to facilitate riding on horseback), which will be necessary on every road to protect your other clothes. Ladies might also consider the "instant dress elevator." This inexpensive item – just 75 cents – can be attached to any skirt, allowing you to raise your hem in a particularly

" We are all very gay and fashionable – exhibiting our diamonds and laces to the eyes of rival mine and millmen's wives and daughters with as much eagerness as would a New York or Parisian belle."

Louise Palmer, "How We Live in Nevada," *Overland Monthly*, May 1869

muddy street. Women planning to visit the California parks will find Yosemite suits for sale in the shops of San Francisco. A bit like "bloomers," these outfits consist of a coat over pantaloons or a divided skirt that can be buttoned back to permit the wearer to ride a horse without a sidesaddle. (Sidesaddles are hard to come by in the wilderness.) But don't be shocked to see women wearing ordinary trousers when they're riding horseback or doing outdoor chores on ranches and homesteads in the West.

WHAT TO TAKE

You can bring a trunk for a long journey by train, but as it's too large to be loaded onto a stagecoach or horse, you'll also need a carpet bag or small valise for shorter jaunts off the beaten track. Experienced travelers recommend carrying soap, brushes, combs, a whisk broom (for dust), a vial of powered borax (to soften hard water), needle and thread, a brandy flask, and small quantities of simple medicines, including quinine and a cathartic compound such as ipecac. Ladies may desire a small bottle of cologne; gentlemen should carry a knife and consider a revolver, depending on their destination and sureness of shot. Although Richard Burton insists on your bringing a hatbox and umbrella, leave them at home, lest they brand you as a tenderfoot and make you an obvious target for practical jokes.

A word about money: Remote mining camps without banks may still depend on gold dust as a medium of exchange, but coins and greenbacks

OPPOSITE Heads (left) or tails (right), a gold eagle is worth $10, and is generally preferred to paper currency. Certainly it's easier to use than the pinches of gold dust that once bought drinks and other goods in rough-and-ready mining camps.

A BIT ABOUT MONEY

Coins rather than bills are the currency of choice in the West, though there are exceptions. One traveler in 1872 made a point of saying they took greenbacks in Utah, and added that in California you could exchange greenbacks for gold notes, which are "more convenient than coins and just as serviceable." Throughout the region, you'll find the national bird has given its name to legal tender: An eagle is a $10 gold piece, while a double eagle is worth twice as much. You can use half eagles ($5) and quarter eagles ($2.50) too.

Spain's monetary legacy lives on in the "bit," which was originally equal to a silver real, or one-eighth of a peso. (Hence the old term "pieces of eight.") To Americans a "bit" means an eighth of a dollar, or 12.5 cents. Since there is no actual one-bit coin, you can get away with a dime, sometimes called a short bit. A long bit is 15 cents. Two bits, though, is unquestionably "a quarter" (25 cents).

And someone who palms off a wooden nickel on you? Well, he's a two-bit chiseler.

should now be accepted in most places, so bring an adequate supply. Beyond that, don't burden yourself with valuables, as stagecoaches and trains may occasionally be the targets of gangs of outlaws. The Deadwood coach, well known for carrying mine profits and payrolls, has been robbed several times; Sam Bass preyed on the railroads around Fort Worth before he was apprehended; and Jesse James and his associates are still at large.

FINDING SUPPLIES

If the first establishment to go up in a Western town is the saloon, the next is undoubtedly a general store. These mercantiles stock every imaginable good and then some, crammed on floor-to-ceiling shelves. In Deadwood, for

example, one visitor was struck by a shop that had "clothing heavy and light, hardware, tinware, mess-pans, camp-kettles, blankets, saddlery, harness, rifles, cartridges, wagon-grease and blasting powder, India-rubber boots and garden seeds, dried and canned fruits, sardines, and yeast powders." If you need replacements for shoes, clothes, or equipment, you'll undoubtedly find it here. These all-purpose stores eventually give way to more specialized shops, as boot-makers, jewelers, drygoods merchants, milliners, and tobacconists arrive to offer their own fine wares.

IF YOU GET SICK

Since the standard of medical care leaves something to be desired, it's a good thing the West is known for its healthful climates. California has long been recommended for its curative powers, and promoters are now touting the atmosphere in New Mexico and Colorado as a remedy for everything from dyspepsia to pulmonary disease. If you're under the weather in a remote

> " The climate of Colorado is considered the finest in North America, and consumptives, asthmatics, dyspeptics, and sufferers from nervous diseases, are here in hundreds and thousands, either trying the 'camp cure' for three or four months, or settling here permanently. "
>
> Isabella Bird, *A Lady's Life in the Rocky Mountains*, 1879

location and can't locate a doctor, you can at least take comfort from the fact that hundreds of others have flocked to these very spots to rest and recover.

If you find yourself near a military installation, the doctor there will often treat travelers for a small fee. You can be fairly certain of their abilities. Army doctors are usually better trained and have passed more rigorous examinations than civilian medical men, who may double as veterinarians and coroners. (Wags like to say they bury their mistakes.)

By all means, carry your own portable first-aid kit. But be leery of "Indian medicines," which are likely the concoctions of snake-oil salesmen. And don't give in to the blandishments of quacks who advertise potions like "DR. SALFIELD'S REJUVENATOR: This great Strengthening Remedy and

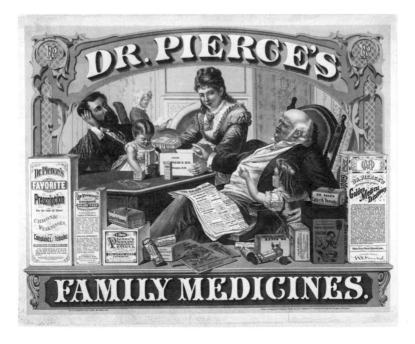

Verve Tonic." Chances are the only thing it will rejuvenate is the manufacturer's bank account.

WISDOM OF THE EAST

Thanks to the thousands of Asian workers who came to toil on the Central Pacific Railroad, there's a Chinatown in almost every Western settlement, though usually not in the most fashionable neighborhoods.

The rail line is finished, but the Chinese have stayed on to seek their fortunes. Some still prospect for silver or gold at mine sites. Others serve as cooks and expert laundrymen. Among their businesses you may also find a herbalist or apothecary. If you're feeling poorly, don't be shy about paying the shop a visit.

After all, there was a reason the Chinese laborers fell ill less often than other railway workers. Chalk it up to their diet of rice, fish, and vegetables – and their habit of drinking hot tea instead of unboiled ground water. Herbal medicine has a long tradition in the Orient, and though an apothecary's jars and bins may be full of odd-looking roots, barks, gums, nuts, flowers, and even powdered animal substances, his prescriptions are much more likely to be effective than the so-called "Indian Medicine" compounds manufactured in the American East.

ABOVE A Chinese railway construction crew takes a break from its labors on the Union Pacific line.

BRINGING BACK SOUVENIRS

The West is full of little treasures, man-made and natural, that are unlike any *objets* you'll find in the cities of the East. Look for Indian artifacts – buffalo robes and moccasins with beadwork, which you'll find more comfortable than any slippers you may have ever owned. You may be able to buy or trade for bags, bows, pipes, quivers, or Indian-made curiosities such as turkey-wing fans, bowls carved out of tree roots, and deer-horn spoons. In the Southwest, keep an eye out for Indian pottery and weavings, which resemble works of art more than utilitarian goods.

Salt Lake City is home to the Women's Union, which sells the handiwork of Mormon wives. Shoes, bonnets, straw hats, artificial flowers, laces, and silk fabric manufactured in Utah are all easily transported home.

Visitors to the Rocky Mountains often are taken by pieces of petrified tree stumps, which preserve the grain and color of wood in a pretty mass of solid stone. At Yellowstone National Park the concessionaire will arrange to have a small basket or bunch of twigs encrusted with minerals deposited by Mammoth Hot Springs as a memento.

Photographers have opened studios in almost every corner of the West. H. B. Calfee's summer establishment is a collection of tents in Yellowstone's Upper Geyser Basin. Why not take home a panoramic picture of the place you've visited. Or have your own studio photograph taken, perhaps wearing a borrowed cowboy hat and bandanna for effect.

ABOVE Jake Gold's Old Curiosity Shop in Santa Fe is stocked with Indian artifacts. This image by William Henry Jackson shows why the street it's on is called "Burro Alley."

4

ENTERTAINMENTS AND VICES

SALOONS

You'll never want for liquid refreshment in the Wild West. Wherever a few people have put down roots, someone has opened a saloon, even if it's merely a board laid over two upended barrels. As soon as there's a main street in town, the thirst parlors multiply quickly behind the wooden false-front façades. Leadville alone had 120 saloons last year, as its local newspaper reported (or perhaps boasted); Virginia City claims 100, while Fort Worth lists about three dozen.

Miners, cowboys, businessmen, and ranchers can belly up to the bar – twenty-four hours a day, in some places – and name their poison: Taos Lightning, Tarantula Juice, Red Eye, or, most often, just plain whiskey. There is beer, too, whose shipment to Dodge City was heralded by the press: "A young lady, Miss An Heiser, is stopping in the city at present. A great many gentlemen have called upon her and express themselves well pleased with her general appearance. The only criticism we have heard made is that the length of her neck is a little out of proportion to that of her body."

" The Comstock is an improving place to live on…. We have more saloons to the population than any place in the country. Every Sunday when there is a show in town we have a matinee and an evening performance. On the Sabbath, also, we are entertained with a horse-race or a fight between a bulldog and a wildcat. "

Gold Hill News, December 7, 1876

There are drinking establishments for every level of society, beginning with one- and two-bit saloons, which often issue tokens in those amounts, good for a short beer each. Don't expect too much in the way of decoration, though, unless you count sawdust, bullet-holes, and broken glass. Some saloons actually stage official boxing matches (as well as animal contests), though it might be hard to tell the difference from the informal slugfests.

At the other end of the spectrum are the exclusive gentlemen's watering holes. The Cheyenne Club, the Washoe Club, and the Carbonate Club, for example, are luxuriously appointed with Brussels carpets on the floor and crystal chandeliers hanging from the ceilings. These elite clubs cater to their wealthy members with imported libations, aromatic cigars, and private rooms for poker.

BAD BEHAVIOR

Liquor, gambling, and the love of a woman have led to more than one fatal fight from the cow towns to the gold fields. Inside the saloons and out on the street, many a frontier lawman has made his reputation – and some have lost their lives – when guns were drawn to settle a score.

In the early days of Virginia City, the *Territorial Enterprise* regularly reported bar stabbings and shootings – including one that took place because one man danced with another's sister and kissed her in a "sportive manner." In Tombstone the Cosmopolitan Saloon was the site of a lethal contretemps over a chambermaid, while shots are frequently fired in the Oriental because of disagreements over cards. And in one legendary shootout in Abilene some years ago, Marshal Wild Bill Hickok was confronting a gambler named Phil Coe, when his friend and special deputy Mike Williams stepped into the line of fire and died. No one held it against Wild Bill, but the town didn't renew his contract, and he had to move on.

The best advice? Keep your gun holstered and all your nasty comments to yourself. Be careful who you dance with – or kiss – and if you happen to insult anyone, be sure to smile.

In between are countless places to share a bottle with friends. There may be music to raise your spirits as you lift the glass, and many places offer billiard tables. In Fort Worth, this can be a surprisingly dangerous game, since the cowboys who frequent Hell's Half Acre sometimes "shoot pool" by firing bullets to propel the balls into the pockets.

"Bucking the tiger," gamblers try their luck at faro in a Cheyenne saloon. Everyone is welcome, as long as they have cash in hand.

GAMBLING

Along with sampling the booze at the local saloons, you can test your luck on games of chance. "Gambling ranges from a game of five-cent chuck-aluck to a thousand-dollar poker pot," one reporter noted about Dodge City's offerings, which are matched in towns throughout the West. The gaming tables are open day and night, with hopeful fortune seekers trying to "buck the tiger" at faro, and more timid souls betting on the numbered balls in a game of keno. Spanish monte is popular in the Southwest, while roulette wheels spin in the fancier gambling dens of Fort Worth.

TIGER, TIGER

From Dodge City to Tombstone, enter any saloon and you're likely to find a faro game. More popular than keno, or the new card game called poker, faro is often announced by a sign depicting a tiger. Why? Some early cards were decorated with pictures of the big striped cat, and faro players are therefore often said to be "bucking the tiger," or "twisting the tiger's tail."

In theory, there's not much to the game. There's usually a green cloth with images of thirteen cards, and you place your bet – a "check" – on the card you think will appear of out the brass dealing box. But the pace is fast and the nuances many. Each round consists of two dealt cards. A wager on the first card goes to the bank. Players collect if their card is second. You can also "heel" or "string along" with more complicated wagers that involve combinations or groups of cards.

Keep an eye on the casekeeper, who records the play on a little counting frame with miniature cards. Meanwhile, a lookout will sit in to keep an eye on you as the casekeeper collects the wagers and pays out any winnings.

Don't count on getting rich. It's a rare faro bank that's completely honest. But often, as one Mississippi gambler lamented some thirty years ago, "It's the only game in town."

" Round the long, green tables are grouped such picturesque and
savage figures as only a frontier town can show: the stalwart scout
in his fringed suit of buckskin, weather-stained and soiled; the
long-booted miner… "

Frank Leslie, *Across the Continent*, 1878

Just about anywhere there's a table and chairs, you'll find poker. Be fore-
warned that the card games attract professional gamblers who can play for
hours or even days. If you find yourself with aces and eights, you might cash
in your chips – literally – as that's the bad-luck hand that Bill Hickok was
holding when Jack McCall gunned him down four years ago in Deadwood.

In the daylight hours, there are horses to bet on. Even if no track exists
for purebred contests, you can often watch locals stage races by spurring
their ponies down the main street.

THEATERS AND OPERA HOUSES

All it takes to turn a thirst parlor into a theater is a stage at the back of the
room. Quick as a wink, the saloon becomes a variety house, welcoming
comics, singers, and musical revues. The quality of the talent varies widely,
but the crowd is usually appreciative, like the audience of cowboys described
by one jaded correspondent: "broad felt hats bobbed approval in unison of
the vile jests upon the stage, and gave the effect of a bed of toad stools, while
half a dozen worn-out graduates, male and female, of Eastern 'vaudevilles'
made up the company."

In more elaborate theaters you might sit in a box looking down at the
stage from the side at entertainments that range from trapeze artists in silken
tights and spangles soaring above the spectators to an off-key vocalizer, such
as Miss Viola de Montmorency, the Queen of Song, whose voice, according to
one listener, "might have had stitches in it, and been none the worse."

Other venues cater to legitimate theatricals, with fare appropriate for a
feminine audience – such as dramas, comedies, and uplifting lecturers.

A performer commands attention – of a sort – at a well-decorated variety theater in the West. Boxes above the stage afford a good view, if you're willing to extend yourself.

There are also the fancier opera houses, though Mozart and Bellini are rarely on the bill. Piper's in Virginia City, which holds special ladies' nights, is almost always thronged with patrons, while the Tabor in Leadville takes the prize for poshness.

Comedians like Eddie Foy and actors like Jack Langrishe have built up reputations throughout the West, traveling from Dodge City to Tombstone, or from Deadwood to Denver and beyond. But the touring performer everyone still remembers is Adah Isaacs Menken in *Mazeppa*, wearing a nude-colored body stocking and not much else as she galloped up a stage-set mountain, strapped to a black stallion.

*"*At each side of the hall are tiers of boxes…these boxes are closed in, and have each a window, through which the inmates must project head and shoulders if curious to witness the performance on the stage; but, as they contain tables and chairs, it is possible that a glass of wine or lager and social intercourse may be more the object than spectacular entertainment.*"*

Mrs. Frank Leslie, *California: A Pleasure Trip from Gotham to the Golden Gate*, 1877

As for theatrical depictions of the West, those have been mostly destined for patrons east of the Mississippi. Buffalo Bill Cody, for one, has trod the boards there in larger-than-life retellings of his own exploits as an Indian fighter. Rumor has it that he's thinking of a new kind of touring extravaganza, set in outdoor arenas and complete with Indians, sharpshooters, and stagecoach robberies. Now that would be a real Wild West show!

DANCEHALLS AND SOILED DOVES

If a glass or two of whiskey makes you want to kick up your heels, the dancehall – or hurdy-gurdy – is your answer. The barman will be serving drinks, musicians will provide the tune, and there will be members of the fairer sex waiting to take a whirl with you. The management may decree, however, that you have to buy a token, and probably a drink, before the lady will step out onto the dance floor.

OPPOSITE TOP Burlesque actresses show a lot of leg in an ad for alcoholic libation.

BELOW Dancing damsels are the attraction at a hurdy-gurdy, though dancehalls rarely call for such formal finery.

"The whiskey soon limbers them up and the motley crowd vie with each other in showing their own peculiar fancy steps, while their partners, the frail sisters of the town, put on their sweetest smiles and enter into the amusement with vigor."

Deadwood Black Hills Daily Times, October 2, 1877

FAMOUS NAUGHTY LADIES

The locals call them soiled doves, prairie nymphs, frails, Cyprians, nauches, calico queens, and the demimonde, but the residents of the bawdy houses have equally inventive nicknames for themselves.

One well-known Dodge City belle is Squirrel Tooth Alice, named for her pet rodent. Her Dodge City compatriots include Cuttin' Lil Slasher, Hambone Jane, and Dutch Jake. Other trail towns boast Sweet Annie, Wicked Alice, Fatty McDuff, Peg-Leg Annie, Kitty Kirl, Roaring Gimlet, a tall gal called Timberline, and the naturally blond Cotton Tail. In Ellsworth, a nymph called Prairie Rose must have been imagining a Western version of Lady Godiva when she sauntered down the main street clad only in a pair of loaded pistols.

RIGHT Squirrel Tooth Alice, one of Dodge City's well-known ladies of the evening, sits for a studio portrait with her namesake animal on her lap.

Dotted among the saloons and gambling dens are other places to find female companionship, from fancy parlor houses and bagnios to bare-bones cribs. Their ladies of the night are sometimes labeled "soiled doves," but they can be tough birds – scrapping in public over money and men. The "frail sisters" lead hard lives, and more than one has been known to seek an early exit through opium or laudanum. From time to time local clean-up campaigns shut the bawdy houses or haul in the girls of "the line" before a judge. Cynics claim, however, that morals have nothing to do with it, pointing out that the fines and court fees keep civic coffers filled.

PRACTICAL JOKES

Try to fit in as you might, you'll probably be spotted as a dude as soon as you arrive in town. That means you'll be fair game for some Western humor, such as trying to make a tenderfoot dance by shooting at his feet!

You may get an invitation to go hunting for quail or snipe. Expect to be left in some remote spot after nightfall, with instructions to listen for sounds of your prey till the wee hours of the morning. Be assured that your companions will be back at the bar, snickering at your gullibility, long before you realize that no amount of snooping will turn up a snipe.

Laugh it off and buy a round when it's your turn. Before you know it, you'll be joining in to welcome the next newcomer in frontier style.

" A 'tenderfoot,' that is, a new arrival from the East, green in the ways of mountain life, they consider fair game for tricks and chaff. "

Ernest Ingersoll, "The Camp of the Carbonates: Ups and Downs in Leadville," *Scribner's Monthly*, October 1879

5

PASTIMES AND CELEBRATIONS

LODGES AND FRATERNAL ORGANIZATIONS

Though you may not know a soul anywhere in the West, chances are good that you have a "brother" there. Virtually every town is home to one or more fraternal organization. The Masons, the Odd Fellows, the Knights of Pythias, and the Elks all maintain lodges for mutual support and civic endeavors. There are gala social occasions, too, like the Masonic ball reported by the Leadville *Chronicle*: "An artistic eye had amused itself, decking the tables with flowers and vegetables grotesquely carved in imitation of many emblems of the order. Mammoth cakes were Masonic with compasses and squares."

If you belong to one of these groups, seek out a meeting, a dinner, or a benefit; you'll be a welcome guest. If you're not a lodge member, you might turn to one of the ethnic or religious organizations that sponsor everything from athletic clubs to drinking societies. Virginia City's roster alone lists B'nai B'rith, the British Benevolent Association, the Italian Benevolent Society, Friends of Poland, the Scandinavian Society, the Swiss Helvetia Society, and the Welsh Club. Don't forget about the temperance groups, which offer more sober entertainments.

RIGHT A compass, one of the emblems of the Masons.

MUSICALES AND "LITERARIES"

" There will be dancing at the Quarters of Lieuts. Chase and Hardy
3rd Cavalry at 8 o'clock pm this evening. All Gentlemen and Ladies
desiring to send refreshments, may be assured that they will be
properly looked after. "

Commanding Officer, Fort Laramie, February 24, 1879

When theater companies are not in town, Westerners stage their own entertainment. If you visit an army post, you're likely to be invited to amateur
theatricals, impromptu lectures, and musical evenings – and you certainly

shouldn't miss the sunset dress parade, where buglers or a band herald the end of day.

Elsewhere, watch for announcements of dramatic readings and discussions of the political questions of the day, sponsored by literary societies. If you're invited to a dinner at someone's home, you very well might spend part of the soiree gathered around the melodeon for a song or two. Some towns have organized amateur brass bands, which with hardly any prompting will meet in the square for a serenade. Musicians who are interested in joining in are usually welcome to hop on the bandwagon and play along.

" The Bel Esprit held its regular weekly meeting last evening…. The entertainment consisted of essays, readings, recitations and music. The first, entitled 'Literature and Arts of Greece'…was a finished and scholarly production…A poem entitled 'Cleopatra' was recited…with excellent effect. "

The [Leadville] Chronicle, December 18, 1879

HOSE COMPANY COMPETITIONS

With their crowded streets and hastily erected wooden buildings, it's no wonder that so many Western towns succumb to fire. It's far more surprising that any actually survive. If they do, it's thanks to the members of hose companies who race to the scene. These firemen take pride in their speed and strength, and most companies show off their prowess during races and contests during the year.

The men are generally decked out in finery for parades, but they strip to tights when it's time to compete. Local companies challenge each other or race against teams from neighboring towns. Deadwood fields a hose

OPPOSITE A Fourth of July celebration brings out the brass as the Cornet Band C Company poses among the rocks in the mining community of Georgetown, Colorado.

Deadwood, Dakota Territory, boasts an all-Chinese hose team for firemen's competitions, though it's unlikely they wear gaiters and skimmers during actual fires.

company completely composed of Chinese-Americans. In Leadville, mine owner Horace Tabor has headed the subscription to send the "fire laddies" of Tabor Hose Company No. 1 to the state competition. Georgetown, Colorado, claims a practical honor: Thanks to the efforts of its four fire companies, the town has never burned down.

ROUNDUPS

After the work of *rodeo* – or rounding up cattle, in the language of the old-time *vaqueros* – is done, the cowboys like to show off a little. If you're lucky, you might get to watch them as they try to outdo each other with exhibitions of roping, riding, or breaking wild horses.

These informal events have begun to give way to organized contests with prizes. Almost a dozen years ago, in Deer Trail, Colorado, a British horseman won a suit of clothes for his skill and was dubbed "Champion Bronco Buster of the Plains." More recently, a Denver reporter attended a roundup show and marveled as a cowboy attempted to ride a horse that had "all four legs bunched stiff as an antelope's, and back arched like a hostile wildcat's." The rider responded by digging in his spurs and using a keen stinging quirt, a forked whip favored by cowboys. "It was brute force against human nerve. Nerve won."

BASEBALL

Professional baseball players may populate diamonds in the East, but in the West the sport is the realm of amateurs. Army posts field teams, and towns stage games in summer and on holidays – even at Christmas in Arizona Territory, where Yuma, Prescott, and the little outpost of Phoenix have all had matches. The kranks, or fans, turn out in droves – gentlemen and ladies alike – to cheer on their favorites.

Fort Worth has its Panthers; Virginia City has its Silver Star club. The latter hoped it might take on the Cincinnati Red Stockings when the professional players made a cross-country tour in 1869. Alas, the visitors never stopped in Nevada, and Virginia City's nine instead had to make do with a match with Carson City. Adding insult to injury, the Silver Star lost its luster that day, trounced by Carson City 54 to 17.

" The baseball fever has flashed forth in this city in all its fury. Among the contests of yesterday was one…between the city nine, all employees of Major James' works, and the Picks. Five innings were played and the James boys beat. *"*

The [Leadville] Chronicle, July 7, 1879

THE HOLIDAY SPIRIT

Christmas in the West tends to be a time for feasts. The tables groan with roasted fowl, sausages, tinned oysters, pickled goods, and other special dishes, as well as fine pastries and candies. Holiday balls and dances at home usher in the New Year. It's a rollicking time for you to visit, as the *Leadville Daily Democrat* reported of this year's festivities: "At 12 midnight, guns boomed, whistles blew, prisoners marched through the streets, happy over their liberations, every saloon did a prosperous business, variety theaters were crowded, merry sleigh riding parties flitted through the streets, and prayers ascended from the watchers in the Methodist church."

All those celebrations pale, however, before the exuberance of the Fourth of July, when everyone young and old turns out for a parade and a picnic. Expect long tables laden with bountiful fare, and a concert by the town brass band. You can listen to speeches, sing hymns and patriotic songs, and watch (or join in) the games: baseball, horse races, hose competitions, boxing matches, foot races, wheelbarrow races, sack races, and more. Don't be surprised if someone sets off a cannon at noon or a six-gun in the evening. And be sure to stick around to admire the fireworks at night.

Just four years ago, the Glorious Fourth marked a century of U.S. independence. Could anything more soul stirring possibly take place ninety-six years from now?

Fowl is fare at holiday celebrations, which call for meat roasted on a spit, often served up at community picnics.

★ 6 ★

PEOPLE TO MEET

WILLIAM F.
"BUFFALO BILL" CODY

You can't separate William Cody from the West: his nickname itself is a symbol of the plains. And what a showman! He's been bringing tales of his frontier adventures and Indian encounters – in entertaining, if somewhat factually suspect, re-creations – to enthusiastic theater audiences for almost a decade.

Cody was born only just west of the Mississippi, near LeClaire, Iowa, in 1846. The family moved to Missouri and then to Kansas. By 1857 Cody's father had died and young Will was working with a freighting outfit, headed for Fort Laramie with a wagon train. His autobiography, published last year, credits him with an entire cavalcade of daring feats during that period, from riding for the Pony Express to gold prospecting in Colorado. It certainly makes for an exciting narrative, though only Cody himself knows how much of it is true.

By 1864 he was back home as a young enlistee in the Seventh Kansas Volunteer Cavalry, but his exploits had barely begun. He met a St. Louis belle named Louisa Frederici, and when the Civil War was over, they married and had a daughter, Arta. To support his small family, Cody tried his hand at running a hotel and founding a town, but mundane business was never his

" To describe the play [*The Scouts of the Prairie*] and its reception is alike impossible....Everything was so wonderfully bad that it was almost good.*"*

New York Herald, April 1, 1873

forte. Instead he turned back to the plains and in 1867 began hunting buffalo, shooting 4,280 animals in eighteen months to feed the railroad workers who were laying track across Kansas. William Cody had become "Buffalo Bill."

As the railroad work ended, Cody worked for the army, scouting, hunting, and, though a civilian, sometimes taking part in the skirmishes that made up the Indian wars. He was with the Fifth Cavalry in 1869 when he met Ned Buntline (real name Edward Z. C. Judson), who just happened to be in search of a main character for his next dime novel. Buntline had to look no further. Less than a year later, *Buffalo Bill: The King of the Border Men* was an overwhelming success.

Buffalo Bill's family increased along with his fame: a son, Kit Carson, named for the renowned New Mexico frontiersman, and a daughter, Orra, were born in the next few years. When the Russian Grand Duke Alexis came to hunt buffalo in 1872, Cody accompanied him as scout and guide, along with George Armstrong Custer.

The wild frontier was tame, however, compared to the next test Buffalo Bill faced: the theater critics of New York and other Eastern cities. *The New York Herald* described him as as "a good-looking fellow, tall and straight as an arrow, but ridiculous as an actor," and dismissed his first vehicle, a melodrama penned by Buntline called *The Scouts of the Prairie*, as "about everything in general and nothing in particular." Cody played himself in a cast that included the playwright and another frontier hero, Texas Jack Omohundro. A year later Cody recruited his old friend Wild Bill Hickok

The "Scouts of the Plains" don urban attire during their theatrical tour in 1873. From left to right: Wild Bill Hickok, Texas Jack Omohundro, and Buffalo Bill Cody.

to join the production, now revised as *The Scouts of the Plains*, though Wild Bill's acting reportedly left a lot to be desired. Eastern audiences received the play much more enthusiastically than did the critics, and melodrama after melodrama, staged by Cody's own touring "combination," has followed ever since.

In the summers Cody has returned to the West and the Fifth Cavalry, where epic and sad events have overtaken him. His son Kit died in 1876, the same year that Custer made his last stand against the Indians at Little Bighorn. Later that year, Buffalo Bill fought and killed Yellow Hair, a Cheyenne warrior, at Warbonnet Creek. The episode – culminating in Cody's claiming a "first scalp for Custer" – is now part of yet another Buffalo Bill theater piece. But Cody's rancor against the Indians is gone. If you attend one of his performances, you'll see real Sioux on the stage, and when the showman speaks, you'll hear him defend the tribes who have tried to retain their territories.

Buffalo Bill is an unforgettable figure in his voluminous mustache and flowing hair, wearing buckskins and brandishing a gun, and he's bringing the Wild West to you.

WYATT EARP

He's been the quintessential Western lawman: strong, silent, and slow to pull his gun. And though he's currently without a badge, he probably won't be for long.

For the past year Wyatt Earp has been in Tombstone – along with his brothers Virgil, James, and Morgan, and his companion, Mattie Blaylock – where he has invested in mining claims and a gambling hall and tried his luck at the faro tables. But he's also worked here for a few months as a deputy sheriff, the profession he's been known for in other Western towns.

Wyatt Berry Stapp Earp was born in Monmouth, Illinois, in 1848 and named after his father's commanding officer in the Mexican–American War. The family soon moved to Iowa; then, during the Civil War, they

*"*It wasn't considered policy to draw a gun on Wyatt unless you got the drop and meant to burn powder without any preliminary talk.*"*

Dodge City Times, July 1877

headed out for a farm in California. Young Wyatt didn't take to agriculture much, however, and left the homestead to try his hand at freighting. He drove wagons as far as Salt Lake City, but when his father took the family back east to Lamar, Kansas, Wyatt wasn't far behind.

By 1870 he was newly married and a town constable in Lamar, but the tranquil times were not to last. His wife died that year, and following a brawl, Wyatt was on the road again, first sowing wild oats in Indian Territory, then hunting buffalo for a season or two. It was at that time, on the Salt Fork of the Arkansas River, that he struck up a friendship with the brothers Ed and Bat Masterson, who, like Wyatt, were destined to wear a lawman's star.

Meanwhile, thousands of Texas cattle were just beginning to be herded north to market. Ellsworth was among the first Kansas towns to entertain the thirsty cowboys with liquor and gambling – and also among the first places to have to deal with drunken troublemakers as a result. Legend has it that Wyatt was on the scene during one brouhaha and was able to talk a gun-toting gambler into surrendering without a shot.

His reputation spread, and by 1874 he was keeping the peace in Wichita, another Kansas frontier cow town. For two years he fearlessly disarmed rowdy cowboys, arrested drunks, and chased a horse thief or two. Then in 1876 he moved on to Dodge City, the wickedest cow town of them all, where he nevertheless enhanced his renown for enacting justice without having to

Lawman and gambler Wyatt Earp has turned his hand to several professions, but he's best known for keeping the peace in several Kansas communities. Serious and steady, he bides his time in Tombstone, Arizona, along with his brothers, Virgil, James, and Morgan, and friends like Doc Holliday and Bat Masterson.

fire a gun, periodically leaving to chase train robbers or pursue other business ventures.

He also honed his gambling skills and attracted some of the West's most famous names to the town's faro tables. Doc Holliday, whom Wyatt had met a year or two earlier, rode into Dodge and hung out his dentist's shingle. Gambler and lawman Luke Short arrived in town soon thereafter, as did Bat Masterson and his brothers, Ed and Jim, who all did their bit to help keep things quiet.

But perhaps Wyatt felt he was performing his job too well. As Dodge City began to settle down, he began to cast his eye further southwest, to the challenges of disorderly Tombstone. Can he make a success of it there, too, without a real gunfight to his name? Only time will tell.

WILLIAM BARCLAY "BAT" MASTERSON

When actor Eddie Foy arrived in Dodge City in 1878, one of the first people he met was Ford County sheriff Bat Masterson. Foy saw a trim, good-looking young man, with a nice face and a well-shaped mustache, wearing his bowler hat at a jaunty angle and toting two silver-mounted, ivory-handled guns tucked into his belt.

He may have looked like a dandy, but make no mistake: Bat Masterson is tough, and at just twenty-five, he has already survived some dangerously close calls.

His parents christened him Bartholomew when he was born in Quebec in 1853, but he never liked the name. Instead he called himself William Barclay. Friends and opponents alike knew him as "Bat."

His family – including three brothers and two sisters – moved several times, to farms in New York and Illinois before finally settling near Wichita, Kansas, in 1871. That year, Bat and his older brother, Ed, began working as buffalo hunters, providing meat and hides to Kansas merchants. The boys

" Bat is well known as a young man of nerve and coolness in cases of danger. He has served on the police force of this city…and knows just how to gather in the sinners.**"**

Dodge City Times, October 13, 1877

wintered on the Salt Fork of the Arkansas River – where they made the acquaintance of Wyatt Earp – and spent a season working as graders for the railroad before picking up their rifles to shoot buffalo once more.

Bat was at a hunters' camp near Adobe Walls in Texas – really not much more than a saloon and a general store – when Indians attacked. Several hundred Cheyenne, Comanche, and Kiowa charged the tiny settlement in June 1874, killing two of the defenders and keeping twenty-eight men and one woman under siege for several days. Eventually the Indians withdrew, and Bat, unscathed, moved on.

He drifted in and out of Dodge City, spent time as an Army scout and teamster, learned to hold his own at the gambling table, and continued to

hunt buffalo. That's what he was doing in 1876, in Sweetwater, Texas, when danger again reared its head. This time it was in the form of a drunken soldier, angry over losing to Bat at cards, or annoyed by his attentions to a certain lady of the evening. When the couple went into a dancehall, the soldier pulled out his gun and opened fire, killing the woman and badly wounding Bat in the abdomen, though the latter managed to get off a mortal shot in return.

Bat returned to Wichita to recover and was still using a cane when he got back to Dodge. Despite the rumors to the contrary, he didn't get his nickname for his habit of

Ever dapper, Bat Masterson often sports a bowler – as well as a cane – as he pursues his fortunes at Tombstone's gaming tables.

using the cane to "bat" his adversaries into submission, though he didn't shrink from a fight either. It wasn't long before he was battling gunslingers and other desperadoes as an officer of the law. In 1877 Bat ran for Ford County sheriff, a post he won by just three votes.

For the next two years, there was plenty to keep him busy, from train robbers and horse thieves to obstreperous cowboys, including one who killed his brother Ed, also a lawman. Bat worked with Wyatt Earp as well, backing up his fellow peacekeeper more than once. Nevertheless, Bat lost his bid for re-election at the end of last year. So now he, too, has gotten out of Dodge.

Bat has caught up with his old pals in rowdy Tombstone and for the moment is seeking his fortune at the gaming tables. If you stop in at the Oriental Saloon, you might find him dealing cards. Rest assured, however, you haven't heard the last of him yet.

CHIEF JOSEPH OF THE NEZ PERCE AND SARAH WINNEMUCCA OF THE PAIUTE

With most Indians now moved to reservations, the debate has begun over the broken promises and outright mistreatment they have suffered at the hands of the U.S. authorities. Although they cannot speak for every tribe, two individuals have emerged as passionate advocates for their people. You may encounter them on your travels; listen carefully to what they say.

Hinmahtooyahlatkekt – Chief Joseph of the Nez Perce – was born in 1840 in northeastern Oregon, in a fertile valley edged by mountains and the mighty Snake River. He grew up in a tribe that had always been proud of its friendly relations with the white man. But pressure to sign treaties and cede their territory eventually divided the Nez Perce. Some bands gave in and were relocated; others, including one led by Chief Joseph's father, resisted and continued to call the Wallowa Valley home.

Chief Joseph of the Nez Perce, with family members, in Leavenworth, Kansas, far from his band's traditional homeland in the Wallowa Valley of Oregon.

They couldn't hold back the tide of settlement forever. A few years after Chief Joseph succeeded his father, the group was ordered to leave for an Idaho reservation on barely thirty days' notice. Other leaders suggested fighting back – but Joseph counseled peace, and it seemed for a while as though that would prevail.

Fate decreed otherwise. While the tribe debated, a few young warriors killed several whites, and the Nez Perce fled toward Canada beyond the reach of the U.S. military. For three months and 1,400 miles, the 700 Nez Perce evaded the army, skirmishing, retreating, fleeing, advancing, and

> **"** Let me be a free man – free to travel, free to stop, free to work, free to trade where I choose, free to choose my own teachers, free to follow the religion of my fathers, free to think and talk and act for myself – and I will obey every law, or submit to the penalty. **"**
>
> Chief Joseph, speech at Lincoln Hall, Washington, D.C., January 14, 1879

fighting again, until they were just 40 miles from the border. In the Bear Paw Mountains, on October 5, 1877, their path was finally blocked. With the other chiefs killed and the tribe ragged and starving, Joseph surrendered in a memorable speech: "The little children are freezing to death. My people…have no blankets, no food…I am tired; my heart is sick and sad. From where the sun now stands I will fight no more forever."

Although the Nez Perce were promised a home in the north, they were actually shipped to Leavenworth, Kansas, and then to Indian Territory, where many more of them have now sickened and died. Chief Joseph himself has traveled to Washington, D.C., to plead their case, and notables and ordinary folk alike come to hear him speak. But does anyone really listen?

Meanwhile, a Paiute Indian woman's voice has also been raised in a plea for justice. Thocmetony – known as Sarah Winnemucca – was born around 1844, in what is now Nevada. Her father, Chief Winnemucca, counseled against trusting whites, but her grandfather, Chief Truckee, held a more conciliatory view. The old man made sure the girl was educated in an army household, where she learned English and Spanish as well as several other Indian languages.

When the Paiute were relocated to reservations in Nevada and Oregon, Sarah was with them as an interpreter for the Bureau of Indian Affairs. Soon she was writing letters to protest the actions of corrupt Indian agents. In 1878, when Bannock Indians fled their reservation, she translated for the army troops who brought them back. Since then she has spoken out more widely and even taken her case to Washington, D.C. "Sarah Winnemucca, now in San Francisco, is good looking," noted a *Washington Post* reporter recently, "with resolute expression and self-possessed manner." Seek her out, and she'll tell you quite clearly what life among the Paiutes is like today.

★ 7 ★

PEOPLE TO AVOID

BILLY THE KID

He's now known far and wide as Billy the Kid, but that's a fairly new nickname. It's merely the most recent alias used in an infamous criminal career, which has been surprisingly long for someone who's just twenty-one.

Billy started life as Henry McCarty, born in 1859 in New York City to an Irish widow. By the time he was thirteen, he was in New Mexico with his mother, brother Joe, and stepfather Bill Antrim. His mother died of tuberculosis less than two years later, and his stepfather barely paid attention when Henry committed his first petty theft – stealing butter from a ranch and selling it in town.

A boyish prank or irrevocable first step to perdition? Either way, the clever, good-natured adolescent quickly followed it up by breaking into a Chinese laundry with a friend and stealing a bundle of clothes. Henry landed in the hoosegow but escaped by wriggling up a chimney, setting a pattern that has gotten him out of some serious scrapes.

Henry – he now used the surname Antrim – headed for Arizona Territory, where he and a pal stole saddles and blankets and a horse or three. He was caught more than once but always managed to get free, either by talking his way out or slipping away.

Meanwhile, his boyish looks enhanced his reputation for charm. Fluent in Spanish, he danced, joked, and courted the eager señoritas of the territory. But Henry had a temper and had learned his way around a gun. Wiry and quick, in August 1877 he got into a bar fight with a blowhard who taunted him over his size and appearance. Henry Antrim – now sometimes called "the Kid" – pulled out his pistol and killed the bully. Self-defense or murder?

He didn't wait around for a jury to decide and took off back to Lincoln County, New Mexico, where a war was about to begin.

The Lincoln County War was a local battle for power and money, to decide which big ranch business would get to supply the army with meat and goods. The fighting was brutal and bloody. The Kid, who now styled himself William H. Bonney – no one really knows why – signed on as a cattle guard and gunman and did his share of fighting.

By the summer of 1878 he was drifting again with a group of friends who rustled cows and stole horses as far as the Texas Panhandle, and he'd

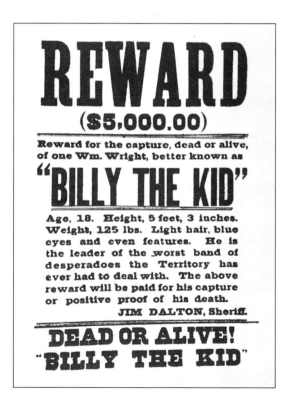

Offering a big reward for an elusive outlaw, the poster lists yet another alias – and a shorter height – for the young Billy the Kid.

" He is about five feet eight or nine inches tall, slightly built and lithe…looking like a school boy, with the traditional silky fuzz on his upper lip; clear blue eyes, with a rougish snap about them; light hair and complexion…He is, in all, quite a handsome looking fellow. "

Las Vegas [New Mexico] *Gazette*, December 28, 1880

earned two indictments for murder. So when an amnesty was declared for those who'd taken part in the Lincoln County War, Billy Bonney was not included. Ever resourceful, he tried to trade information for a pardon, but politics prevented a deal that stuck. Last year Billy testified in territorial court, then managed to elude those who wanted to see him behind bars. On the run again, he rustled cattle, ran a gambling table, and generally raised enough hell to earn a $500 bounty on his head, inspiring reporters from New Mexico to New York to dub him "Billy the Kid."

Now, thanks to newly elected sheriff Pat Garrett, Billy the Kid has finally been apprehended and is once again in jail. We all know that Billy's a slippery character. Any bets on how long he'll remain behind bars?

GERONIMO

For more than twenty-five years, the fierce Apache have alternately warred and made peace with the other inhabitants of Arizona and New Mexico territories. They have attacked, been brutally assaulted, and have retaliated with equally vicious force, as one chief after another has stepped forward to lead them. The man to watch now is Goyahkla –"One Who Yawns" – a Bedonkohe Apache whom the Mexicans dubbed "Geronimo" (possibly invoking St. Jerome in Spanish) after a particularly bloody battle in 1851. With other warriors, he had fought to avenge a massacre by Mexican troops who killed twenty of his tribe in a quiet camp – including his own wife and children – while the men were trading horses in town.

No written records exist, but it seems Geronimo was born around 1823, near the Middle and West Forks of the Gila River. Moody and intelligent, he grew to be a skilled hunter and an adept war leader, as well as something more: a medicine man who had the power to evade bullets, heal others, and see things happening miles away. For decades he remained off center stage, raiding in Mexico during the 1850s and fighting alongside other Apache chiefs – Mangas Coloradas and the great Cochise – in the 1860s. In 1872 Geronimo followed Cochise to the new Chiricahua reservation in south-eastern Arizona. Perhaps the younger man continued to ride into Mexico, too, to steal ponies or carry out his continuing desire for revenge.

After Cochise died in 1874, the over-the-border raids proved to be useful ammunition for the army officers who wanted to move Geronimo's band of Apaches to another reservation. In 1876, when authorities tried to do just that, the One Who Yawns woke up. He bolted, taking 700 other Apaches with him in the dead of night. Their flight struck terror into residents of the

Geronimo (on horseback, wearing a bandanna) has led his Apache followers on raids throughout Arizona Territory, stealing horses and leaving dead men in his wake.

territory, as Indian raiders killed men and made off with countless horses. An ambitious young Indian agent named John Clum (who has since moved into journalism as publisher of the *Tombstone Epitaph*) took off in pursuit with a cadre of Indian policemen. On April 21, 1877, he caught up with Geronimo and transported him in shackles to the San Carlos reservation, along with some 500 other members of his tribe.

Geronimo mouldered in prison for two months and then, surprisingly, was released. He remained at San Carlos, however, while other Apaches, led by a chief called Victorio, began to wreak havoc along the Rio Grande. In April 1878, Geronimo finally fled, taking refuge in the Sierra Madre Mountains, joining Victorio in combat, and sometimes attacking on his own.

Last year he voluntarily returned to the reservation, while Victorio was hunted down and killed. There Geronimo remains, at least for the moment. The medicine man has always seen his own future path, and only he knows where that will lead. Like a kind of war cry, his name signifies battle, and if Geronimo strikes once again, you do not want to be in his way.

JOHN HENRY "DOC" HOLLIDAY

Though Doc Holliday does have a degree in dentistry, you might look for someone else if you find yourself with a toothache in Tombstone, Arizona. Just don't tell him that to his face. The mercurial dentist is known for his quick temper and his even quicker hand with a knife or a gun. And he's not someone you want to cross when he's downed one whiskey too many.

A delicate blond, blue-eyed native of Georgia, John Henry Holliday was born in 1851, attended dental school in Pennsylvania, and then hung up his shingle in Atlanta. Not long after, however, he was diagnosed with the consumption that carried off his mother when he was fifteen. He sought a new climate and eventually fetched up in Dallas, where for five years he continued to clean teeth and fill cavities – though some say he left more than one bullet hole in men he disagreed with. As his health worsened, his gambling improved, and increasingly he could be found in a saloon at the faro or

DENTISTRY
J. H. Holliday, Dentist, very respectfully offers his professional services to the citizens of Dodge City and surrounding country during the summer. Office at room No. 24, Dodge House. Where satisfaction is not given money will be refunded.

advertisement in the *Dodge City Times*, June 8, 1878

poker table. His days as a church-going Methodist and a member of a temperance organization were long over.

Continually in trouble, Holliday moved from one rough-and-tumble town to another, through Colorado, north to Wyoming and perhaps the Dakota Territory, or south to New Mexico, and back to Texas. By then he had taken up with a hot-tempered Hungarian-born prostitute known as Big Nose Kate Elder. Her real name is Mary Katherine Harony, and she and Doc have had a stormy on-again, off-again relationship that continues to this day.

The couple were in Fort Griffin, Texas, in the winter of 1877–78, when Wyatt Earp came through from Dodge City. It was probably then that he and Holliday became acquainted, the first step of an unlikely but enduring friendship.

What happened next is the stuff of legends. They say Holliday was at a faro game with a local tough who kept fiddling with the "deadwood," as the discards are known. When the player wouldn't stop, Holliday simply collected the wagers and was about to leave, until his opponent threatened him with a gun. The dentist responded with a fatal knife slash to the belly. It was self-defense, but a local lawman locked Holliday up in a hotel room anyway. When angry townspeople began to gather, Kate came to Holliday's defense. She lit a fire in a shed to distract the would-be lynch mob, then freed her lover, and they fled. Is the story true? Maybe… or maybe not.

In any case, by June Doc and Kate had arrived in Dodge. Holliday again advertised his dental services and helped Wyatt Earp out of at least one tight

The doctor is in…in Tombstone, that is, though John Holliday has now given up the practice of dentistry.

situation with a bunch of drunken drovers. But he couldn't make a go of it. Later in the year Holliday was on the move again. In Trinidad, Colorado, he is said to have faced a gambler called Kid Colton in a showdown that left the young man dead in the street. So it was on to Las Vegas, in New Mexico Territory, now a booming rail town on the old Santa Fe Trail. This time Holliday's stab at practicing dentistry lasted only a few weeks. He then bought a saloon.

He was restless and courted trouble, gambling, arguing, and drinking to ease the pain of his worsening consumption. Some say he dined with Jesse James and Billy the Kid in July 1879 at the hot springs on the edge of town. He may have tried the faro tables at other places. But he was in Las Vegas when a disagreement proved fatal for local gunman Mike Gordon. Some time after that, Wyatt Earp and his family stopped in town on the way to the territorial capital of Prescott. When the group left, Holliday and Kate were with them.

Holliday liked Prescott well enough to stay after the Earps had moved on to Tombstone. All winter you could find him in the Palace Bar or one of the other saloons on Whiskey Row. But Tombstone was calling, and a few months ago he arrived in the wide-open mining boomtown, where he seems to have settled in. Kate comes and goes and is often in residence at Fly's Boarding House, next to the O.K. Corral. Holliday makes his living at faro and drinks heavily, despite the cough that wracks his frail body. On occasion he helps Wyatt and his brothers uphold the law, but more often than not, he bends it.

Take the recent contretemps in the Oriental Saloon, when his argument with another gambler and the saloon owner turned ugly. Shots were fired; men were wounded. The drunken Holliday was cold-cocked with a pistol and eventually fined $20 and $11.30 in court costs.

If you meet him, give him a wide berth. Doc is a legend in his own time, but he writes a repeat prescription for trouble.

JESSE JAMES

Now you see him…now you don't. For three years after the attempted robbery of the First National Bank of Northfield, Minnesota, on September 7,
1876 – and the capture and conviction of his associates, the Younger brothers
– the infamous outlaw Jesse James and his brother, Frank, managed to lie low.

Were they in hiding? Were they using fake names? Were they looking for
new targets? In towns all over the West, people were eyeing
strangers and wondering if the James brothers were planning a raid on the local bank. Last June in Leadville,
Colorado, *The Chronicle* reported seeing the pair "in
conversation with other desperadoes in the most public places in the city." And rumors were rife that not
long after that Jesse had dined with Billy the Kid in Las
Vegas, New Mexico.

What's certain is that Jesse James resurfaced with a new
gang in October 1879 at Glendale, Missouri, to relieve a train
shipment of some $40,000. He followed up that deed a few months ago by
robbing a stagecoach in Kentucky. Where will it end?

The beginning, at least, is fairly well known: Jesse James was born in
1847 on the family farm in Kearney, Missouri. Frank was four years old at
the time. The boys' father, Robert James, died in California's Gold Country
in 1850, but their mother, Zerelda, would marry, be widowed, and marry
again – to Reuben Samuel – within just a few years.

During the Civil War this part of Missouri was a vicious killing field, and
the James-Samuel family were fervent Confederates. Frank joined William
Quantrill's Raiders and participated in savage attacks in Kansas, while Jesse
saw his stepfather tortured by Union soldiers. By the time he was sixteen,
Jesse, too, had become a "Bushwacker," as Missouri's Southern-sympathiz-

Baby-faced Jesse James poses for a portrait in 1864; since then he's become a hardened
bank robber.

" These bold fellows only laugh at the authorities, and seemingly invite their sleepy enterprise, by bearding the legal lion in his lazy lair. **"**

Lexington [Missouri] *Caucasian*, August 30, 1873

ing guerrillas were known. For the James brothers, rebellion didn't end with the surrender at Appomattox. After the war, resentful of Reconstruction, and furious at those who didn't share their pro-slavery views, they turned their attention to criminal activity that was daring, lucrative, and deadly.

Jesse, Frank, and the Younger brothers began with the Clay County Savings Bank, in Liberty, Missouri, on February 13, 1866, making off with almost $60,000 in broad daylight but killing a bystander in the course of the crime. For the next decade, they roamed from Missouri and Kansas to Kentucky and Iowa, pulling other bank heists and robbing railroad express shipments, stagecoaches, and even the Kansas City Exposition Ticket Office. All the while, a Missouri newspaperman extolled the gang's exploits, and neighbors covered up their whereabouts, protecting them from the posses on their trail.

In 1874 Jesse married his first cousin, Zerelda Mimms, and Frank also took a wife. Yet domestic life never seem to interfere with the train robberies. By then the men of Pinkerton's National Detective Agency – motto: "We Never Sleep" – were chasing the gang. The pursuers blundered badly when they surrounded the James home on January 26, 1875. Thinking Jesse and Frank were inside, the detectives tossed an incendiary device through the window. The explosion killed Jesse's half-brother, shattered his mother's right arm, and led to renewed sympathy for the outlaws. Jesse and Frank continued their illegal rampages, turning their sights north to Minnesota.

The abortive Northfield robbery was the end of the James–Younger gang, and the beginning of Jesse's association with a different kind of confederate, who didn't share his Civil War experiences. They say this new band of thieves sometimes quarrels among themselves. For Jesse that may also prove to be the beginning of the end.

Even in his early days as a dime-novel hero, Buffalo
Bill wore his hair long and his mustache full. The
outfit this illustrator dreamed up for him might
not have lasted long on the plains, but the scene has
captivated thousands of enthusiastic readers.

Charles Christian Nahl and August Wenderoth painted miners in the Sierra Nevada in the early 1850s, when prospectors from around the world were still flocking to the gold fields of California and a fortune could be made with a pick and shovel.

ABOVE Intimidating mountains lie ahead in Albert Bierstadt's *Surveyor's Wagon in the Rockies*, in which the painter captures the loneliness of the enterprise along with the fearful expanse of the Western landscape.

OVERLEAF Fort Laramie's first incarnation was a palisaded fur-trading post called Fort William, which was what painter Alfred Jacob Miller saw when he traveled through Wyoming Territory in 1837.

Old Faithful shoots skyward in a delicately tinted watercolor by Thomas Moran, who accompanied the Hayden Expedition to Yellowstone in 1871. The artist's images boosted sentiment for the creation of a national park.

★ 8 ★

MUST-SEE SIGHTS

DEADWOOD, DAKOTA TERRITORY

Don't be confused if someone in Deadwood warns you about the dangers of the Badlands. They don't mean the rugged, dry hills of the Dakota Territory, but the lower end of Main Street, where saloons, dancehalls, theaters, and sporting houses form a rough district irrigated by a constant flow of alcohol.

To be sure, some of the "anything-goes" attitude of the lawless – and illegal – mining camp has dissipated in the four years since prospectors named this long muddy gulch after the dead trees on the surrounding slopes. And the devastating fire that started in the Empire Bakery last fall eliminated pretty much all of the ramshackle frontier structures that had housed Deadwood's early drinking and gambling establishments. However, since their thirsty clientele have remained in town, local entrepreneurs have responded with newer, bigger, and sturdier places of business.

The most famous of all is Nuttall & Mann's Saloon No. 10, now located across the street from where it was on August 2, 1876, when Jack McCall interrupted Wild Bill Hickok's poker game by shooting the famed former lawman in the back of his head. Hickok was holding pairs of aces and eights, which gamblers have taken to calling the "dead man's hand." The victim's funeral was one of the town's first big occasions, with everyone turning out

" The streets are daily crowded with busy people quite as much as with loafers and idlers…. The mud on Main Street is knee-deep and to cross over anywhere else but on the two or three plank crossings is almost a matter of life and death.*"*

Sidney [Nebraska] *Telegraph*, May 22, 1877

ABOVE *Harper's Weekly* depicts Deadwood in October 1876 as an upstart Black Hills mining settlement where shacks are set up willy-nilly, almost in the middle of the road.

to see Wild Bill laid out in his handsome coffin, with his "long chestnut hair, evenly parted over his marble brow, hung in waving ringlets over the broad shoulders," according to a reporter for the *Chicago Inter Ocean.*

Another newly rebuilt watering hole is the lavish Gem Variety Theatre, whose proprietor Al Swearengen has been in town since its earliest days. The *Black Hills Daily Pioneer* described his original Gem as "neat and tastefully arranged as any place in the West." It was, in fact, a notorious dancehall, bar, and bagnio, where Swearengen installed young ladies he lured from Chicago and points east with promises of a career on the stage. He's continued those nefarious practices in his spacious new quarters on the same spot.

The popular Bella Union, though, has closed its doors. Now a grocery store occupies the main floor while a meeting hall fills the space above. It's sorely missed, not only for its variety acts, dancehall, and gambling, but also for the occasional real-life melodramas that took place there. Like the time

OPPOSITE After a fire swept through the settlement, Deadwood was rebuilt with more permanent buildings.

an actor named Banjo Dick Brown shot and killed Ed Shaunessy, his lady love's former paramour, who'd attacked him with an ax.

Even without the Bella Union, there are enough bars and bawdy houses to give you a feel for what Deadwood was like when miners worked their placer claims right on Main Street, pulling out $200 or even $2,000 worth of gold with their sluice boxes and rockers. Nowadays the important mining takes place a few miles away in the little town of Lead, in underground operations like the Homestake Mine, which George Hearst bought for $70,000 a few years ago. But the miners come to spend their money in Deadwood, where prizefights, dogfights, cockfights, wrestling matches, card games, and

faro aplenty are available to part them from their earnings, while the hurdy-gurdy places are lively with dancing till the wee hours of the morning.

Since the fire, Sol Star and Seth Bullock, pillars of local society, have rebuilt their hardware store on Main Street. Star, a former city councilman, was recently named postmaster, while Bullock, who served as county sheriff for a year, has also started a livestock outfit and a flour mill with his partner.

As Deadwood has taken its place as the county seat, it's become "the center of business operations in the Black Hills," according to the *Sidney Telegraph*, "the market from which all outlying mining camps are supplied with groceries, provisions, miners' supplies, wet grocers, etc." A host of mer-

SACRED BLACK HILLS

For the Sioux, the Black Hills of the Dakota Territory are sacred ground, revered in myth and crucial to their way of life. The land was guaranteed to the tribes as their home and hunting ground by a treaty signed at Fort Laramie in 1868, but half a dozen years later there were already rumors of gold in those hills. In 1874, George Armstrong Custer led an expedition with the official mission of finding a spot to locate a fort; unofficially his troops – which included engineers – were scouting for the precious metal. When they found it, the fact was duly reported by the journalists who also rode with the expedition.

A year later a party of scientists went back to assess the extent of the ore, and by then some 4,000 prospectors had already illegally entered the area. As the government scrambled to try to buy the land from the Sioux, and the military attempted to discourage further settlers, the Indians left the reservation, clashing with the army in several places and defeating Custer at the Battle of Little Bighorn. The tribes couldn't hold out forever, though. By 1877 the Sioux had been sent to other reservations, and the government declared the Dakota Territory open to settlement.

In reality, the miners had already moved in, creating the town of Deadwood in April 1876.

" To witness a dance at one of our hurdy gurdy houses, we think would be interesting to some of our Eastern friends unaccustomed to such scenes, particularly after the dance has been under way for several hours, and the participants in the dance have had sufficient time to become well filled up with the choice brands of whiskey usually sold at such places. *"*

Deadwood Black Hills Daily Times, October 2, 1877

cantile establishments offer clothing and food (though admittedly fruit and produce are hard to come by). The Stebbins & Post Bank will exchange your gold dust for greenbacks at $18 an ounce. Al Merrick publishes notable events in the *Deadwood Pioneer*, one of the two daily newspapers in town, though town gossip also is broadcast by telephone. It costs just 25 cents to place a call from Deadwood to nearby Lead on the recently installed telephone exchange.

It's easy to find your way in town. Main Street stretches for a mile along Deadwood Gulch, forming an upside-down Y with Sherman Street, which runs along Whitewood Gulch. The genteel residential neighborhood of Forest Hill has developed above Main Street, along terraced avenues crossed by narrow stairway passages that lead down to the businesses. On flatland just east of Sherman Street is the gracious enclave of Ingleside. And at the center of it all stands the stark Congregational Church, where several denominations hold Sunday services according to a carefully worked-out timetable.

There's a thriving Chinatown as well, beyond the Badlands. Among the laundries and exotic herb shops is merchant Wing Tsue's emporium, which offers an intriguing array of Oriental goods – silk, china, and ivory items – in a store redolent of sandalwood and teak.

You'll have no trouble finding a room. You can stay at the venerable IXL Hotel, where the first ball for respectable society was held a few years ago, or get a room at the Wentworth Hotel for about $3 a day. The most reliable kitchen, until recently, was under the direction of Lucretia Marchbanks at the Grand Central Hotel. Since the fire, though, that inn is being renovated as a lodging house. If you want Aunt Lou's famous biscuits, you'll have to seek her out in Lead, where she's now cooking at the Golden Gate Mine.

TWO DEADWOOD LEGENDS

They rode into town together, part of the same wagon train that arrived in July 1876, and even then their reputations were already larger than life. Dime novels had turned Wild Bill Hickok into a fictional hero performing impossible deeds, and a series featuring Calamity Jane was soon to follow.

Their real stories, though, are memorable enough. Born in Troy Grove, Illinois, in 1837, James Butler Hickok had been a spy and scout for the Union during the Civil War and later served as a lawman in Kansas, though his quick hand with a gun – he shot perhaps ten men over the years – caused townspeople to ask him to move on. After his exploits were publicized in the late 1860s, he even toured with Buffalo Bill Cody in a Wild West theatrical. But an actor's life was not for him. Hickok returned to the frontier, where he indulged his penchant for whiskey and cards. In April 1876 he married Agnes Lake Thatcher, who managed a traveling circus, but he left her behind to join the new gold rush in Dakota's Black Hills.

Martha "Calamity Jane" Canary was born in Missouri, probably in 1856, and came west with her neglectful parents and a few siblings a dozen years later. She grew up tough on her own, with a vocabulary of swear words that rivaled any bullwhacker's (a profession famous for foul language). The exact reasons for her nickname are lost in time, though she certainly has had her share of bad luck, undoubtedly brought on by an inordinate fondness for alcohol and the company of unsavory characters. She's been known to put on men's buckskins or a private's uniform and join a soldier's expedition, and she's spent time entertaining boys in blue at the "hog ranch" near Fort Laramie. That's where she joined Hickok and his pal Charlie Utter on the road to Deadwood. After she arrived, she kicked up her heels in dancehalls and cooled them in jail. But she's also pitched in to nurse ailing miners during times of sickness.

Calamity Jane has had several husbands – legal and not. Was Wild Bill among them? No. Only their legends have been intertwined.

Finally, keep an eye out for Calamity Jane, though you may hear her colorful exclamations before you spot her (probably heading for the nearest saloon). If she ever dictates her memoirs, they'll make a rollicking read, though you may not want to wager on their reliability. Rumor has it she wants to be buried next to Wild Bill, whose grave was recently moved to the new Mount Moriah cemetery. It's a peaceful, quiet spot, where you can contemplate a Wild West town that's been anything but.

ABOVE The fateful moment: Jack McCall shoots Wild Bill Hickok in Saloon No. 10.

RIGHT Calamity Jane in her preferred garb.

DODGE CITY, KANSAS

" Dodge is the Deadwood of Kansas ... her principal business is polygamy without the sanction of religion; her code of morals is the honor of thieves, and decency she knows not. *"*

The Hays City Sentinel, 1877

It's easy to ride the Atchison, Topeka & Santa Fe Railway right into Dodge City. Every day a train pulls into the dusty west Kansas cow town whose reputation for iniquity has been proclaimed far and wide. You may already have heard the story about the steely-eyed conductor on the line who confronted a cowboy with rotgut whiskey on this breath but no ticket in his pocket: "Where are you goin'?" the conductor asked. "Goin' to Hell," said the cowboy. "Then give me a dollar, cash," came the reply, "and get off at Dodge."

The first thing you'll probably notice as you step off the depot platform – along with a sign warning you not to tote your six-shooter in town – is the mountain of bones beside the tracks. No, they're not the remains of unlucky gunfighters. Those are buried in Boot Hill. These skeletons belonged to buffalo, and the animals are one of the reasons that Dodge City was founded here less than a decade ago.

Buffalo hunters worked on the plains throughout the 1860s, shooting the creatures for meat, robes, and sport. After 1871, when someone figured out how to use the hides for leather, the hunt turned into wholesale slaughter. Bat Masterson and his older brother, Ed, were among those who came with powerful .50 caliber Sharps rifles to shoot the buffalo and skin the carcasses for the traders.

Meanwhile, as railroad tracks were pushing westward across Kansas, a handful of entrepreneurs realized that this site, just a few miles from Fort Dodge and on the new Santa Fe line, had real possibilities for prosperity.

OPPOSITE Piles of buffalo bones attest to the slaughter of thousands of animals on the Western plains, as workers cure and stack the hides. Dodge City got its start as a shipment point for the skins. As the animals were eradicated, the industry collapsed.

FRENZENY & TAVERNIER

THE MOVING END OF THE TRAIL

The first cattle drives, after the Civil War, moved huge herds of Texas beef to army forts and Indian reservations in New Mexico and Colorado. But in the 1860s, as the railroad extended west, ranchers instead drove their herds to the new railway cattle depots, which gave them access to eastern markets.

The Shawnee, Chisholm, and Western Trails are just three of the best-known routes, which had multiple cutoffs and branches. At trail's end towns sprang up to capitalize on the cattle business, to say nothing of the cowboys. At first city fathers courted the drovers with handbills that touted their new cattle pens and fair beef prices. But the Texas longhorns also carry a tick that infects domestic cattle. One by one, the towns have set up quarantine lines that push farther and farther west.

Abilene was one of the first trail towns to prosper. In its heyday, it was as wild and wicked as Dodge. After Abilene banned cattle drives, Waterville, Junction City, Chetopa, Coffeyville, Salina, and Solomon each had a run as Queen of the Cow Towns. Newton lasted just one season; Ellsworth and Wichita carried on for five years. Now it's Dodge City's turn to reign.

After all, the buffalo hide dealers needed a way to ship their booty, and at Fort Dodge, the post commander had just outlawed alcohol. Surely off-duty soldiers would welcome a place to drink. In June 1872, as the first ladles of whiskey were dispensed from a tent here for two bits a shot, a township company was formed to lay out Buffalo City, later renamed Dodge.

Alas, the buffalo hunters did their work too well. As the herds diminished, eliminating the source of sustenance for many Kansas Indians and pushing the tribes into reservation life, Dodge City's newfound livelihood began to disappear, too. In 1873 buffalo traders had loaded 754,529 hides onto Santa Fe Railway boxcars. By 1876, the animals were virtually gone.

There was still plenty of grass on the plains, however, more than enough to feed the thousands of cattle that were soon being driven north from ranches in Texas to Kansas railheads. Dodge welcomed the herds, and the men who accompanied them.

READING THE SIGNS

On the open range and during cattle drives, ranch owners keep track of their cattle with brands, supplemented by cuts on a cow's ear or dewlap. Brands can use letters and numbers, which might be shown "reverse," "crazy" (upside down), "lazy" (on its side), "rocking" (on a curved bar), "tumbling" (tilted forward), or "swinging" (hanging from a curved bar), to name just a few. There can be geometric signs, like circles, bars, stripes, diamonds – in whole, halves, and quarters – or stylized pictures of an arrow, a hat, a sun, or a heart, among many others. You read the brands like hieroglyphics or heraldic devices, in a certain order, noting the symbols from left to right and top to bottom.

But woe unto anyone caught with a running iron, used to blot brands, in his gear. Such a "brand artist" might find himself invited to a necktie party, in which he'll be the one swinging.

Cracking their whips and spurring their steeds, cowboys drive a herd of longhorns down Dodge City's main street.

Every summer and fall the merchants, saloonkeepers, and professional gamblers eagerly wait for the rambunctious trail riders who hurry to spend their hard-earned cash, first at the bathhouse and barber, then at the haberdasher, and finally in the saloons and dancehalls, at the faro and keno tables, and in the houses of ill repute.

Who are these cowboys? They're young, mostly in their early twenties, and a fair many of them are black or Mexican. They dress the part, with spurs, chaps, and ten-gallon hats. They've spent three months on the trail – at $30 a month – with only a head drover, a cook, and ten other men for company, aside from their cow ponies and 2,500 head of cattle. For weeks they've eaten nothing but beef, beans, bacon, and biscuits and slept under the stars.

ABOVE On a quiet afternoon in 1878, George Masterson, another of Bat's brothers, is behind the bar of the Varieties dancehall. On livelier evenings patrons come to watch the can-can.

Can you blame them if they want a whiskey or two – or three or four – and a bit of female companionship?

Watch out late at night, though, when the cowboys have had several shots of the so-called Kansas sheep-dip. Even though they're supposed to leave their six-guns at Ham Bell's Livery Stable for safety, more than one buckaroo has ridden down Front Street at 3 A.M., whooping and hollering and firing off a few rounds in the air.

To keep order, Dodge City has a marshal, along with the Ford County sheriff. In the last few years, Bat Masterson – who began using a cane after he was wounded in the groin during an altercation in Texas but has since found it useful for subduing recalcitrant drunks – served as undersheriff and sheriff, while his brothers Ed and Jim worked in the marshal's office alongside Bat's friend Wyatt Earp. Of that group, only Jim Masterson is left in town. Ed was killed by a drunken cowboy, and Earp and Bat have moved on to Tombstone.

During the day, Dodge usually shows a decorous demeanor. "I was happily surprised to find the place in the daytime as quiet and orderly as a country village in Indiana," one visitor from Kokomo wrote.

The hotels are first-class. The two-story Dodge House, which boasts thirty-eight rooms behind its peaked-roof façade, is the finest in town, with

ABOVE The Dodge House's top-of-the-line accommodations are conveniently located on Front Street, not far from the railroad station and close to Delmonico's Restaurant.

a bar and billiard hall conveniently located next door. (It's where Doc Holliday took up residence when he was practicing dentistry here.) More strait-laced guests prefer the Great Western Hotel, run by the teetotaling Dr. Samuel Galland, whose wife serves up buffalo and venison for dinner.

The businesses on the north side of Front Street – the respectable side of the tracks – provide pretty much everything you need. You can't miss Mueller's Boot Shop: there's a giant boot outside. It's such a lucrative business that the owner has started building a new residence out of stone. Frederick Zimmerman purveys guns, ammunition, and hardware behind an impressive false-front façade, while Delmonico's proclaims itself the "Restaurant for the Elite." A few doors away, Wright, Beverley & Co. has a new brick building jammed with clothing, groceries, ranch and farm equipment, jewelry, tobacco, and household goods. You'll find dressed chickens for 10 cents a pound, coffee for 25, and oats for 56 cents a bushel. Across Bridge Avenue is McCarty's Drugstore, which doubles as the post office.

To the north, the town's two newspapers maintain rival camps on Chestnut Street. At the *Dodge City Times*, editor Nicholas B. Klaine is likely to inveigh against the town's wicked ways, while at the *Ford County Globe* the editors are less judgmental but no less colorful. When a fight recently occurred between two ladies of easy virtue, the *Globe* titled the story "Scarlet Sluggers" and reported that "Tufts of hair, calico, snuff and gravel flew like fur in a cat fight."

On Sunday, you now have a choice of places to pray: the new Presbyterian Church or the Union Church, which welcomes worshipers of several denominations. Of course, most Dodge visitors don't come for the prayer services. Gamblers, cowboys, and curious travelers alike all want to see the bars, gambling tables, and dancehalls. You'll never go thirsty. Last year the town counted fourteen saloons for its 1,200 residents.

The Long Branch, on Front Street, is the newest saloon owned by Chalk Beeson, who has set it up with a bar and billiard table in front and a separate space for faro and keno. No bar girls will importune you here, but Beeson, who's an amateur violinist, sits in with four other musicians to serenade the drinkers and gamblers. Beeson is even talking about organizing a local band dressed as cowboys and led by a conductor wielding a six-shooter instead of a baton.

Next door is the music-less Alamo – "a quiet, pleasant resort, where the cigar and refreshments can be enjoyed at leisure," according to the *Times*. Beeson's previous enterprise, also on Front Street, is now called the Lone Star, in deference to the Texas cowboys who make up much of the clientele. Or try the Alhambra, one of the gamblers' favorites, owned by local politico James "Dog" Kelley, well known for his penchant for hounds.

Nearer the railway depot is the Occident, recently taken over by Henry Sturm, who advertises "a pint, keg, or barrel of the very best, old Irish, hot Scotch, six year old hand made sour mash Kentucky copper distilled bourbon or old Holland gin."

South of the tracks the scene is more raucous. There you'll find the dancehalls, like the Varieties, where hostesses will drink with you and spend ten minutes with you on the dance floor for 75 cents… and perhaps more time in a horizontal position for an additional fee.

There's the Lady Gay, a boisterous place owned by Jim Masterson and Ed Springer, who also built a theater next door called the Comique (locals pronounce it "Commie-kew"), where dancers and gamblers keep the place lively till the early hours. Actor Eddie Foy graced the boards there for the last two summer seasons. On one occasion when he was performing, and Bat Masterson and Doc Holliday were gambling, a cowboy rode by and shot through the plank wall. "Everybody dropped to the floor at once, according to custom," Foy remembers. "Bat Masterson was just in the act of dealing in a game of Spanish monte with Doc Holliday, and I was impressed by the instantaneous matter in which they flattened out like pancakes on the floor." Wyatt Earp, who was standing outside, managed to cut down the rider with several shots.

Take your cue from Foy. If you hear gunfire, hit the ground. But be aware that Dodge City boys like to play their jokes. Be skeptical if they tell you that someone named Luke McGlue has some lucrative proposition for you. And if you brag about your encounters with Indians, you may find that the "gang" invites you to go hunting, only to be attacked by some spurious locals in war paint. Take it in good grace and offer to buy your companions a drink. Remember, you're in the place *The Kinsley Graphic* has dubbed "Beautiful Bibulous Babylon of the Frontier."

Cowboys push Texas longhorns onto a cattle car in Abilene in 1871. One of the first trail towns to welcome the herds, the community later banned them.

FORT LARAMIE, WYOMING TERRITORY

" A beautiful place for a town [where] the roads from Independence, Fort Leavenworth, St. Joe, Council Bluffs, and the Arkansas River all come together. "

Jesse Morgan, diary

It's a 90-mile stagecoach ride from the railroad stop in Cheyenne, Wyoming Territory, to Fort Laramie, a trip across dry windy plains that will take you a little over a day, with stops for meals and perhaps a rest at road ranches along the way. If you feel like complaining about the discomfort, well, remember what it was like for the thousands of emigrants who trudged or jounced along for 700 miles to reach this spot on the way to what they hoped was a promised land in the West.

Today, of course, your companions may be bound for more earthly entertainments in Deadwood, or for the gold fields of the Black Hills. Even the teamsters are colorful characters. Keep an eye out for Martha Canary – Calamity Jane herself, who's been known to handle the reins on the Cheyenne–Deadwood coach line.

As you near your destination, you'll see Laramie Peak rising 10,000 feet above the grasslands. Indeed, this is where the plains give way to the Rocky Mountains and the clear-flowing Laramie River joins the wide, muddy North Platte. Thanks to the new iron truss bridge, you no longer have to brave a precarious ferry ride or cross a rickety wooden bridge. Instead your coach will clatter across the river under a graceful bow-shaped triple span, and deposit you at the stage stop by the Rustic Hotel.

The actual fort lies just beyond. Don't expect a wooden palisade. Unlike the army posts of popular dime novels, this fort has no outer wall. It looks more like a neat little town than a military encampment. A tidy boardwalk edges the parade ground. Trees shade post buildings, flowerbeds brighten corners, and white picket fences define the front yards of officers' quarters. The civilization of the States has arrived.

What a difference from the scenes that played out at this frontier outpost over the past four decades! It began as a fur-trading post founded by enterprising mountain men in 1834. As the need for beaver pelts waned with changing fashion, the traders bought buffalo skins from Sioux and Cheyenne who came to the new wooden stockade, but within a few years the American Fur Company took over, put up an adobe-walled fort, and carried on the business. Each carefully prepared hide represented hours of an Indian woman's work – stretching, cleaning, tanning, and softening the skin – and was exchanged for perhaps a dollar's worth of goods. (It might fetch four times that back in St. Louis.)

By 1836 other people were stopping at the fort, beginning with the first Oregon-bound missionaries and their wives. Fort Laramie lay directly on the Overland Trail that led to South Pass, the easiest place to cross the Continental Divide. In the late 1840s Mormon followers of Brigham Young adopted this route, and after gold was discovered in California, the trickle of emigrants surged to a flood. Warm weather brought a parade of wagons bearing 50,000 people every summer in the peak years. The white of drying linen would be visible everywhere as women washed their laundry in the river, their first opportunity since leaving Missouri. The fort's wheelwright could help repair broken wagon axles; the blacksmith could forge new iron tires. And at the sutler's store one could replenish dwindling supplies, though everyone complained of the prices, which ran as high as $1 for a pint of flour and $4 for a quart of preserved peaches.

In 1849 the Army bought the trading post – at a bargain price of $4,000 – and gradually let the old structure crumble as new buildings went up around the smart parade ground. In the coming years the infantry and cavalry troops who were billeted here would have a serious mission: dealing with the Indians in both war and peace.

The tribes had begun to chafe at the settlers' encroachment on their buffalo-hunting grounds. The Bureau of Indian Affairs responded by convening a Treaty Council at the fort in 1851. Some 10,000 Indians – including traditional enemies like the Cheyenne and Shoshone and the Sioux and the Crow – set up their teepees on the nearby plains. The Treaty of Fort Laramie, or the Treaty of Long Meadows, as the Indians referred to it, assigned home

A SIDE TRIP TO
CUSTER'S LAST STAND

From Fort Laramie to the battlefield is more than a 300-mile journey, but you can follow the old Bozeman Trail northwest into Montana Territory, past Fort Fetterman and the sites of three other forts abandoned more than a decade ago. Where the Little Bighorn River winds below a low hill, Lieutenant Colonel George Armstrong Custer and 263 Seventh Cavalry troops died on June 25, 1876.

Custer and his men were taking part in a massive campaign to force the Sioux and Cheyenne onto reservations, when they encountered some 8,000 Indians from several tribes, including 2,000 warriors, camped near the river. The weather was hot, and Custer had cut his normally long hair, but wore his customary buckskins. He sent one of his subordinates, Captain Frederick Benteen, and 125 troops, to a ridge to block any Indian escape. When a small group of warriors emerged from the encampment, Custer dispatched Major Marcus Reno and another three companies to chase them. Custer himself was to follow. But those plans were thwarted.

The Indians repulsed Reno's attack and drove the soldiers back into cover. Custer, meanwhile, more than four miles away, charged the overwhelming gathering of Indians with his remaining 200 men. They were quickly surrounded. None would survive the furious, bloody battle.

Benteen eventually came to the rescue of Reno's forces, which had also suffered heavy losses. The next day the Sioux and Cheyenne broke camp and started for the mountains. There was nothing left for the soldiers to do but hastily bury the mutilated corpses of the dead.

Last year the battlefield was declared a national cemetery, though Custer's body and those of several officers have already been reclaimed and buried elsewhere. There's talk of putting up a memorial, but surely no one – white or Indian – will forget the Battle of Little Bighorn.

OPPOSITE Sitting Bull, the well-respected leader of the Hunkpapa Sioux, led his people to safety in Canada after their victory at the Battle of Little Bighorn. He is still living in Saskatchewan, but there are rumors of his imminent return.

areas to each tribe and promised gifts worth $50,000 a year. The peace was tenuous. After only three years an incident over a stray cow set off a pattern of retribution and raids on both sides that went on intermittently for twenty-five years, with breaks for peace councils that brought famed generals and government representatives to meet with respected chiefs at Fort Laramie. The waves of settlers and prospectors, and repeated instances of mismanagement, misunderstanding, and conflicting cultures too often led to deadly discord. Increasingly, the army tried to remove the Indians to reservations by any means possible: enticements, persuasion, or ruthless compulsion.

The last straw came in 1874 with the discovery of gold in the Black Hills, considered sacred land to the Sioux and promised to them as a homeland. When the military failed to halt the stampede of miners, the Sioux and Cheyenne escaped the reservation, and in 1876 the government began a massive campaign to bring the Indians under control. Although the tribes –

led in part by Sitting Bull – had recently annihilated George Armstrong Custer and 263 men of the Seventh Cavalry at the Battle of Little Bighorn, the Sioux and Cheyenne were forced to surrender.

That was just a couple of years ago, but today Fort Laramie is a quiet place, home to six companies with perhaps 350 men, as well as teamsters, wives, and even children. Critics say that the post has outlived its usefulness, but for the time being it's a unique opportunity for visitors to experience army life on the frontier.

A WHO'S WHO OF THE SIOUX AND SOME OTHER PLAINS TRIBES

Many Indian leaders stepped in to guide their people both in battle and in negotiations for peace. Here are a few:

WASHAKIE, a Shoshone chief, supported peace during the council at Fort Laramie in 1851.

CONQUERING BEAR (also called Brave Bear), a Brule Sioux, signed the Treaty of Fort Laramie but died three years later when a disagreement over a cow led to a bloody massacre in which almost thirty soldiers also were killed.

SPOTTED TAIL, another Brule Sioux, began by waging raids in retaliation for the incident in which Conquering Bear died but later argued persuasively for accommodation with whites.

BLACK KETTLE, a Cheyenne chief, sought peace at Fort Weld in 1864. Shortly afterward, his band was slaughtered at Sand Creek by Colonel John Chivington and his men. Black Kettle survived, only to be killed when George Custer attacked the Cheyenne who were camping along the Washita River in 1868.

CRAZY HORSE, a young Oglala Sioux warrior, ambushed Captain William Fetterman's detail of thirty men in 1866 and ten years later took part in the Battle of Little Bighorn. In 1877 he surrendered to government troops at Camp Robinson, Nebraska.

RED CLOUD, a chief of the Oglala Sioux, refused to attend treaty talks in 1867–68 until new forts along the Bozeman Trail were eliminated. Later he took his people to a reservation.

SITTING BULL, a great chief of the Hunkpapa Sioux, became a leader of the Indians who refused to move to the reservations. With 2,000 warriors from various tribes he wiped out more than 200 soldiers under George Armstrong Custer at the Battle of Little Bighorn in 1876. He later escaped to Canada, though some say he may soon return. He'd certainly be a big attraction at any Wild West show.

OPPOSITE Army officers and their friends on the steps of Old Bedlam, the Southern-style bachelor quarters at Fort Laramie and the site of social gatherings on the post.

The wood-frame Rustic Hotel advertises "clean beds and first class meals." Whether it lives up to that claim or not, it's the only public accommodation at Fort Laramie. You might, however, find yourself invited for tea or dinner with one of the officers' families, who occupy more genteel lodgings – mostly cottages divided in two – that are comfortably but simply furnished. It doesn't pay to settle in too deeply; residents can always be "ranked out" by the arrival of a more senior officer.

Enlisted men are housed in long barracks that flank the parade ground, but bachelor officers live in a two-story balconied building that resembles a manse of the antebellum South. Old Bedlam (named perhaps for the revelry that has taken place there) is the social center of Fort Laramie, and with luck you'll be invited to one of the dances that liven up the post's routine.

Be sure to stop in at the Post Trader's store, which continues to provision civilian and soldier alike. It's not much to look at, but this rectangular mish-

" There is a very good store here [at Fort Laramie], but…whiskey could not be obtained without a written order from the Governor. "

William Chandlers, *A Visit to Salt Lake*, 1857

mash of adobe, stone, and logs has been a congenial meeting place for everyone from scout Jim Bridger and newspaperman Horace Greeley to Buffalo Bill Cody, General William Tecumseh Sherman, and Sioux chief Spotted Tail. Inside, the shelves and cases are filled with flour and canned goods, cloth, mirrors, ammunition and guns, and countless other necessities of life on the frontier (including alcoholic libations). Part of the building is set aside for a clubroom with billiards, and there's a post office, in case you want to send a letter home. If you crave fresh bread, head to the post bakery, where loaves for the troops come out of the ovens every day.

Hopefully, you won't need to visit the surgeon, who can be found at the post hospital, though he also keeps an office in his stylish quarters. He's

IN THE TROOPER'S KIT

An enlisted cavalryman gets $13 each month and an ill-fitting uniform that includes a blue wool blouse, sky-blue trousers, gray shirt, boots, and a broad-brimmed slouch hat. On patrol, he carries a carbine rifle and sling, saber (unless it gets in his way), Colt .45 revolver and a cartridge belt, knife and sheath, overcoat, canteen, haversack for food, tin cup, poncho, and forage sack. He loads saddlebags on his horse, and packs a lariat, picket pin, and feedbag, as well as cloth for a shelter.

At mess his company is periodically issued 12 ounces of pork a man, 15 pounds of beans, and 10 pounds of rice for every 100 soldiers. Each soldier's daily 18 ounces of flour goes to the bakery to make fresh bread. He might be able to supplement his meals with canned goods from the trader's store, or with pies and milk sold by the post's laundresses. Of course, he never touches a drop of whiskey. (It is usually at least a glass.) But when the bugler blows "Boots and Saddles," he is always ready to move 'em out.

probably treated fewer arrow wounds than you imagine. "Rheumatism and Bronchitis prevailed as usual in spring time," one doctor reported a decade ago, "cuts, bruises, sprains, and wars making up most of the remainder."

Some of those "wars" probably took place at the notorious Three Mile Ranch, a rough-and-ready "hog ranch" – as these dens of iniquity are known – just three miles off the post, where meals, cigars, and whiskey are for sale, along with female company.

If you keep to the fort, you'll be entertained by a daily drill and a sunset dress parade, with the post band – or at least a few buglers – in attendance, and a single cannon salute. On holidays and other special occasions, you might hear the glee club, attend a lecture, or watch the soldiers participating in a sports competition. Baseball, boxing, and racing are particularly popular. On the Fourth of July, you're likely to enjoy "a salute, an oration, singing, and a grand ball," as one passing traveler did twenty years ago.

Before you leave the post, seek out Sergeant Leodegar Schnyder, the ordnance officer who arrived at the fort when the army first took it over and has been here ever since. He's seen the endless line of wagon trains and stood guard over peace councils. He defended the fort on the single occasion it was raided, and served as postmaster in quieter times. He has married – twice, to army laundresses – and raised three children here. He can tell you what it was really like to witness life in the Old West on the Indian frontier.

"I…applied to Captain Clark, who at once assigned me a room – there being few troops there at present – and for the five days I remained there…I was treated with more than hospitality – with generous kindness."

Horace Greeley, *An Overland Journey
from New York to San Francisco
in the Summer of 1859*

FORT WORTH, TEXAS

" Fort Worth is beautifully situated on a broad plateau. The banks are steep and precipitous, one hundred and ten feet in height, covered with luxuriant foliage. The prospect from this plateau is grand beyond description…during the last year 500,000 head of cattle were driven through Fort Worth on their way to Missouri and Kansas, and as we left the town we met a single drove containing 1,250 head. "

Colonel John Weiss Forney, *What I Saw in Texas*, 1872

Fort Worth likes to boast that it's where the West begins; its sister-city Dallas declares itself the place where civilization ends. Enjoy the tussle for bragging rights as part and parcel of travel in the Lone Star State, where a magazine reporter recently noted that "in the eyes of every true Texan the particular location where he has taken root is the focal attraction, the garden centre of the earth, while the next town is the antipodes of all that is good, great, and prosperous."

No one doubts that Fort Worth has become a "cow town," however. For more than a decade it's been a gathering point for the herds of longhorn cattle about to be driven to markets in Kansas or other points north, and the spot for rowdy cowboys to enjoy one last fling before they hit the trail. Now, with the arrival of the railroads in Fort Worth – first the Texas & Pacific, and then the Missouri–Kansas–Texas line – there's even more reason to bring the cattle here for shipment, and even more cowboys bellying up to the bars and occasionally riding into the saloons on horseback.

You can chalk up Fort Worth's success to its fortunate location, on broad bluffs above the junction where the Clear Fork and the West Fork rivers flow together to form the Trinity. It was a good place to build a fort in 1849, one of a line of defenses stretching from the Rio Grande north to Indian country designed to protect tentative settlements from Indian attacks. The army troopers stayed only a few years, however. By 1853, pioneers had moved further west, so the garrisons did too. As they abandoned the military buildings, townspeople moved in, setting up residences and businesses in the

A bird's-eye view of Fort Worth in April 1876 shows the courthouse and a commercial district along Main Street. The empty blocks filled in a few months later when the railroad arrived.

cabins, barracks, and stables lined up around the parade ground, which has been the heart of the town ever since. It's where a new county courthouse, built of limestone with a cupola-topped dome, went up at the top of Main Street after its predecessor burned down a few years ago. (The story of how Fort Worth won the county seat in the first place is a funny tale involving an election campaign lubricated with a couple of barrels of whiskey near the polling place and perhaps even a dozen voters imported from a neighboring county.)

The town's population began to grow in earnest after 1865, as residents of the former Confederate states painted "GTT" ("Gone To Texas") on their

Life in camp on the trail from Texas often revolves around cups of coffee. Arbuckles' is the cowboys' favorite brand, perhaps because each package contains a peppermint stick.

homes and stores, pulled up stakes, and headed west. Meanwhile ranchers began gathering up the cows that had roamed loose on the open range and figuring out how to get them to market. It wasn't always clear whose cows were whose. There was an abundance of mavericks, as unbranded cattle were called, after the Texas tale of a certain Sam Maverick who neglected to mark his herd and found that his neighbors had claimed the cows for their own.

Fort Worth was the last big town before the Chisholm Trail, which led to the Kansas railheads serving the beef-hungry East. Cowboys would bring the herds here, drive them up Rusk Street and across the Trinity River just east of the courthouse, and bed down the steers for a few days before continuing north. The town flourished; its merchants did good business selling months of provisions for the trail, and found other ways to cater to cowboys and cattle-owners alike. The *Fort Worth Democrat*, under the civic-minded direction of B. B. Paddock, tracked the town's growth in 1873: "Two more

TEXAS LULLABIES

The longhorns that hoof it along the dusty trails can easily be spooked by a storm or a sudden noise. Cowboys have learned to keep the herds quiet by singing – if they haven't already lost their voices whooping it up in town. "The Old Chisholm Trail" is one favorite. "Red River Valley" is another. And there's always "Bury Me Not on the Lone Prairie." Sometimes a wordless mournful melody – a so-called Texas lullaby – is enough to do the trick.

drygoods stores. Two more drugstores. Two more printing offices. Another livery stable. Three brick kilns in progress." There were several banks, a Ladies' Ice Cream Parlor, a competing newspaper in the weekly *Standard*, and plenty of lawyers to go around. Land speculation was fueled by talk of the railroad – an idea Editor Paddock promoted in graphic form by imagining Fort Worth as the central junction of railroad lines stretching outward in all directions. Detractors likened the image he published to a tarantula, but that didn't stop the momentum.

Alas, the national financial collapse of 1873 did. The railroad was put on hold, prosperity retreated, and the town got so quiet that a Dallas wag published a fanciful report in his local *Herald* about a panther being found asleep on the streets of downtown Fort Worth. Well, that woke things up. Town fathers and entrepreneurs embraced the nickname Panther City, putting a feline emblem on the newspaper masthead, naming a fire engine after the animal, and adopting live panthers as mascots. They've even christened the amateur baseball club the Fort Worth Panthers, or, more affectionately, the Cats.

Now with more than 6,000 residents, Fort Worth has certainly livened up again. Aside from the train lines, a stagecoach runs from here all the way to Fort Yuma in Arizona Territory, 1,560 miles away. Hotels vie for the honor of being named the biggest and best. The ninety-five-room Mansion opened in 1876 at Fourth and Rusk Streets, followed two years later by the three-story brick El Paso Hotel at Third and Main, its eighty rooms luxuriously

appointed with walnut furniture and gas lighting. The Peers House, another pleasant hostelry, has advertised that it employs female waiters, whom the *Fort Worth Standard* deems both "ornamental" and "exceedingly useful." You can also find up-to-date accommodations at the Transcontinental, the Virginia House, the Pacific, and the Clark House, which is even nearer the train depot.

If you have an adventurous streak, follow the advice of magazine correspondent Frank Taylor, who observed that "any stranger wishing to rough it

COWBOY LINGO

The Spanish brought the horse to the New World, and their descendants in the Southwest are responsible for many of the practices of today's cowboys – as well as the words they use while riding the range. (No one wants credit for the words they utter in saloons.)

MUSTANG – a wild horse, from *mesteño*, which means "stray"

BUCKAROO – from *vaquero*, which means, literally, "cow man"

WRANGLER – someone who takes care of the horses, from *caballerango*

CHAPS – the leggings that protect a cowboy from painful cactus encounters, shortened from *chaparreras*

TEN-GALLON HAT – from *galon*, the braid that decorated a cowboy's wide-brimmed hat

LARIAT – the indispensable rope was *la reata* in Spanish

DALLY – the looping of a lariat around a saddle horn, from *dar la vuelta*, or "give a turn"

CAVVY – a supply of saddle horses on the trail, from *caballada*

RODEO – from the Spanish word for "encircle," the annual roundup of cattle before a drive, a time when many cowboys can't resist showing off their riding and roping skills.

for a while can readily obtain an invitation to accompany the hardy Texans upon their annual 'rounding up,' which occurs in the early summer, when all the cattle upon a range are brought together, the calves ear-marked and branded, and the selection made for market. The visitor will be expected to provide himself with a pony and equipment. Plenty of smoking and plug tobacco will prove a potent means of ensuring popularity." Those who prefer to remain in town can at least get a close look at the herds that are gathered north of the Trinity – surely a fine spot for a stockyard someday.

Some of the town's best restaurants serve customers twenty-four hours a day. You'll dine on tender steaks, of course, along with frontier favorites such as venison, bear, buffalo, and prairie chicken. You can find a well-set table at the Lafayette Restaurant, Hunter and Sheridan's Saddle Rock Oyster Saloon, and the Delmonico. Order desserts at the Want & Hartsfield Confectionery, and for cigars and newspapers patronize Pendery's Sample Room. You'll find a more extensive choice of reading matter, including seventy-six dailies and weeklies and eighteen monthly magazines, at Harry Cobb's newsstand just a block from the courthouse on Houston Street. All manner of businesses line Houston and Main Streets – including shops for ready-made women's dresses and custom-made men's suits. You can wear the finery to the opera at Evans Hall; the revues and variety shows at the Centennial Theater don't call for fancy clothes. And, sad to say, sartorially anything goes at Fort Worth's notorious watering holes.

Among the oldest of those is the First and Last Chance Saloon, which began as an undistinguished room with raw wooden shelves for libations. Uncle Bob Winders's Cattle Exchange bills itself as the "handsomest saloon in Texas," while the Tivoli offers variety shows, oompah music, and a free lunch at noon. Those with an aversion to wild cats should stay away from the Keg Saloon, which keeps a panther for a pet. The Red Light, on the other hand, is wild enough on its own. Along with the Waco Tap (which recently succumbed to fire), it has been the most notorious of the many raucous bars, dancehalls, gambling dens, and bordellos that liven the blocks between Seventh and Fifteenth Streets and between Main and Jones Streets – Hell's Half Acre, as it's known in Fort Worth, though it actually extends over an area five times that size.

" A dozen or more of the festive cowboys...congregated at the Red Light, and after mounting their horses, each drew his six-shooter, and blazing away in the air, fired twenty or thirty shots, at the same time putting spurs to their horses, they made tracks for the depot, and there reloaded and fired another volley. **"**

Fort Worth Democrat, April 10, 1878

Respectable women – and strait-laced men – should stay away from the district, for within those boundaries a lawless spirit reigns, with fights sprawling out into the streets and cowboys on horseback shooting off their six-guns to announce their arrival, their departure, or nothing at all. The shenanigans got so out of hand a few years ago that voters clamored for reform and elected Tim "Longhair Jim" Courtright as city marshal, and since then the atmosphere has calmed down – at least for a while. Courtright, who has been rumored to run his own gambling tables, was just defeated for a fourth term and is leaving town. Someday, undoubtedly, he'll be back to settle scores. Meanwhile, Hell's Half Acre remains a fertile field for cowboys to sow their wild oats.

LEADVILLE, COLORADO

" [Leadville's miners] have a high regard for a gentleman,
but a hatred of a swell; no objection to good clothes,
but a horror of 'frills'; a high respect for genuine virtue,
but boundless hatred of cant; an admiration for nerve amounting
to worship, but a contempt of braggadocio that often results
in an impulsive puncturing of both the braggart and his boasts. *"*

Ernest Ingersoll, "The Camp of the Carbonates:
Ups and Downs in Leadville,"
Scribner's Monthly, October 1879

Just last year, when the Tabor Opera House opened its doors in the Rocky
Mountain town of Leadville, theater enthusiasts still had to board a stage-
coach for the final dusty leg of their overland journey to get there. No more!
Travelers now arrive comfortably by railroad, merely the latest in a host
of modern amenities that in barely three years have transformed a muddy
Colorado mining camp at 10,500 feet into a notable "cloud city."

Today Leadville boasts gas illumination, a system of water mains and
hydrants, an active fire hose company, and a telephone exchange, which
serve a booming population of perhaps 20,000 souls. The hordes are lured
by improbable but true tales of miners who struck it
rich on silver in a dizzyingly short space of time.
Foremost among those, of course, is Horace
Austin Tabor, formerly Leadville's mayor and
now the state's lieutenant governor. Tabor
and his hardworking wife, Augusta, came
west to try their luck during Colorado's
Fifty-Niner Gold Rush. After unproduc-

Horace Tabor has risen from a would-be miner
to a phenomenally wealthy mine owner,
Leadville mayor, and Colorado politician.

tive claims in several camps, Tabor was running a general store in the almost deserted town of Oro City when a couple of sharp-eyed veteran prospectors realized that the dark, heavy sand clogging up the gold diggings farther up California Gulch was actually a carbonate of lead that was rich with silver. An entrepreneur built a smelter in Leadville in 1877, making silver mining and processing more affordable and lucrative, and a new rush was on.

The Tabors moved their home and store to the new settlement, and Horace immediately became a civic booster. His ability to fund local improvements soared dramatically, however, after he grubstaked a couple of miners, provisioning the men with equipment worth about $60 in return for a third of whatever they found. Their discovery turned out to be the wondrously productive Little Pittsburg Mine, which made Tabor a rich man. He has since multiplied his earnings by investing in other claims, bankrolling commercial buildings, opening an opera house, and founding a bank, to say nothing of his political ambitions.

BENEVOLENT BROTHERHOOD

Like many burgeoning Western towns, Leadville has its share of fraternal organizations. The Masons, the Odd Fellows, even Jewish lodges like B'nai B'rith, have full rosters of members. So, too, does the local Elks chapter. What few residents realize, though, is that English theatrical producer, actor, monologuist, and singer Charles Vivian, a popular figure on the local stage – and who died in Leadville just a few months ago – was responsible for the birth of the Benevolent and Protective Order of Elks.

The group dates to Vivian's days as a young actor in London, where he and a group of friends formed a club called the Jolly Corks. When the thespian arrived in New York, he attached the name to similar gatherings – complete with alcoholic beverages – on otherwise dry Sundays, the actors' only day off. When one of their number passed away, the group provided a burial, initiating the benevolent activities that have distinguished the group, which now has many official lodges, under its new name of Elks.

"The most perfect place of amusement," according to the Leadville *Chronicle*, the ornate Tabor Opera House threw open its doors in November 1879 and now welcomes national entertainers.

With a success story like that, who could blame eager newcomers from envisioning mineral riches for themselves? Everyone in Leadville, it seems, has silver on the brain, and the mining vocabulary colors every aspect of daily life. "The salutation is 'How deep are you?'" a writer has reported. "A man tries a new boarding place and leaves it because it 'doesn't assay well'; forsakes a business because it did not 'pan out enough.'"

The town's reputation has brought sightseers and other curious travelers as well as fortune-seekers and reporters. A couple of years ago, Susan B. Anthony, the well-known champion of women's suffrage, passed through and gave a speech that was surprisingly well-received by her audience of mostly male miners. Buffalo Bill Cody graced the stage of the new Tabor Opera House for two nights, and former president Ulysses S. Grant's visit was a highlight of the past summer.

Meanwhile, Leadville's town fathers and entrepreneurs are working hard to turn their once-ragtag camp into a metropolis worthy of such attention. They've removed cabins and shanties from the middle of stump-filled roads and renamed and regularized avenues and addresses. Harrison Street remains the main north-south thoroughfare, lined with respectable commercial enterprises. The town's finest hotel – the three-story Clarendon, with an elegant barroom, a gentlemen's reading room, a ladies' parlor, and even a barber shop – went up on Harrison Street last spring, followed by the Tabor Opera House next door six months later. The Clarendon is always crowded, it seems. If you can't book one of its 112 rooms (at $4 a day), there are good accommodations to be had at the Hotel Windsor, the Exchange Hotel, or the Grand – Leadville's original hostelry – as well as dozens of simpler boarding houses.

The Clarendon also has a bustling dining room where mines are the usual topic of the day, but the Saddle Rock Café is equally fine, and the Tontine restaurant provides stiff – and stylish – competition. There you are likely to see fashionable Leadville supping on oysters and mountain quail to celebrate anything from a birthday to a bonanza.

The central blocks of Harrison Street and its cross avenues are now crowded with shops and commercial blocks in wood and brick, though visitors continue to remark on the remaining motley canvas-covered tents where some business is conducted. Downtown real estate has become so valuable that even Horace Tabor moved the sturdy house he built in 1877 off the main boulevard and onto East Fifth Street. In general Leadville's residential area has acquired architectural pretensions, replacing old log cabins with homes that boast ornamental cornices, porches, and even paint. Mine engineer August Meyer has put some of his fortune into an elegant two-story Greek Revival dwelling. And a couple of blocks away, the tall spire of the new Annuciation Church – just one of several houses of worship – is already becoming a Leadville landmark.

Shopkeepers have been quick to see the opportunities here. Besides hotels and restaurants, there are, according to a *Harper's Weekly* writer, "five general merchants, four dry-goods stores, ten clothing, eleven grocery, three drugs, four jewelry, six boot and shoe, one commission, three fruit and confectionery, two furniture, five feed and grain, three hardware, and two book and stationery merchants, twelve meat markets...." The list goes on and on. Keeping track of the new business enterprises, as well as mining reports,

A well-appointed apothecary shop has shelves and cabinets filled with the latest remedies and even illumination by gaslight.

accounts of the various fellowship lodges, and society doings, is the *Evening Chronicle*, the town's leading newspaper. If you don't agree with its Republican bent, you may prefer to pick up the *Herald* or the *Democrat*.

The papers also report on the brouhahas that often erupt in the taverns, dancehalls, gambling dens, and brothels that cluster along boisterous east–west Chestnut Street and a block away on Second Street. You'll have dozens of drinking establishments to choose from. There's a saloon called the Little Church Casino for its tall, arched windows, and another ominously named the Bucket of Blood. The Pioneer, does, in fact, date to Leadville's earliest days. There's sometimes even musical entertainment in these establishments, though proprieters don't always vouch for the quality of musicianship. A sign in one popular bar reads: "Please do not shoot the pianist; he's doing his best."

OPPOSITE Couples kick up their heels to the sounds of a fiddle and a cornet in a Leadville dancehall, where a turn on the floor costs 50 cents, cash in hand.

SOME HELP WANTED

Prompted by voluminous mail asking about opportunities – and salaries – in Leadville, the editors of *The Chronicle* have surveyed local job openings and found out what one might expect to earn. A few excerpts from their report:

Competent hardware clerks are scarce and can always get work. They are paid from $75 to $100 per month.

First-class milliners receive from $18 to $25 per week. Such are scarce and hard to get. None but the best should come here, however, as there are plenty of poor ones in the city.

Machinists are paid from $3.50 to $4 per day. Boiler makers get $3.50 per day. There is no demand for these artists and the idle ones are numerous.

The town is overrun with barkeepers of all kinds. Many skillful ones are idle. The salaries paid range from $75 to $125 per month.

Assayers abound in the camp. Those at the mines and smelters get from $125 to $200 per month, according to their knowledge of chemistry.

Faro and other dealers receive $5 per day. The woods are full of them.

The day clerks in our hotels receive $100 per month. They are more polite than those of the East, and it would not do for them to become insolent, as the average carbonate hunter is not slow in pulling the pistol.

The salaries paid writers for the daily papers range from $25 to $40 per week. There is no demand for special articles which are paid for and novelists find no work to do. Reality here reads like wild romance to the outside world. There are scores of journalists in the city waiting anxiously for the time when they will be needed, and we can advise none to come with the idea of engaging in journalism.

That should also be a hint that in Leadville a wardrobe includes a gun. Alas, travelers should be forewarned about Leadville's reputation for lawlessness. Even in its earliest days as a mining camp, Leadville was known for claim jumpers – miners who would move in and take over someone's else's diggings. Later, freighters often carried arms to prevent their shipments from being hijacked. Just last year rumors were rife that Jesse James and a couple of cohorts were operating in the area. And even now muggings and robberies have prompted a committee of vigilance to take action. But don't let it spoil your visit: Simply exercise caution and in the wee hours walk with companions and keep to the middle of the street. The town's too lively for you to stay in at night.

The theatrical scene, for one thing, is not to be missed. The Grand Central, the Coliseum, the Theatre Comique, the Olympic, and the New Leadville stage legitimate plays, performances by noted comedians and singers like Eddie Foy and Charles Vivian, as well as variety programs not always appropriate for family consumption. Leading the list is the three-story Tabor Opera House, built of brick and iron and perhaps the finest venue between St. Louis and San Francisco (at least until Tabor completes the theater he's said to be planning for Denver). The gas-lit auditorium – decorated in red, white, and gold and furnished with scarlet plush seats – was inaugurated

by Jack Langrishe (previously a Deadwood denizen) presenting *The Serious Family*. It continues to show melodramas, farces, comedies, and dramas, all for a tariff of $1.50 on the parquet and 50 cents in the gallery.

On fine summer afternoons horse-racing fans might want to follow the newly improved road west to Soda Springs. The Leadville Trotting and Running Association holds three races a day, beginning with harness contests and ending with a saddle competition.

With its silver an unshakeable pillar of the country's monetary system, Leadville is growing into a major metropolis that surely will soon rival Chicago or San Francisco. There's already a hint of a big-city scandal. You might hear tongues wagging about the separate households that Horace and Augusta Tabor are maintaining, now that they're both spending more time in Denver. In some circles it's whispered that the lieutenant governor is keeping company with his new "Baby," a divorcée named Elizabeth Doe. Someday that story might make the subject of a ballad, or even an opera worthy of his own theater.

Elizabeth Bonduel McCourt Doe has come a long way from Oshkosh, Wisconsin, where she was born in 1854. Recently divorced, she cuts a fine figure on the streets of Leadville.

SALT LAKE CITY, UTAH TERRITORY

" This was fairy-land to us, to all intents and purposes – a land of enchantment, and goblins, and awful mystery. "

Mark Twain, *Roughing It*, 1872

As soon as the Golden Spike was struck near Ogden, Utah Territory, transcontinental rail passengers began arriving in droves to take the spur line south to tour Salt Lake City. What an irony! Who would have thought that the settlement founded by Brigham Young in 1847 as a self-sufficient refuge for his Mormon followers – a New Jerusalem apart from other states – would turn out to be such a tourist attraction?

But even before trains made cross-country travel easy, this outpost in a fertile valley, shielded by the Wasatch Range and bordered by alkali plains, had already begun to attract outsiders' attention. Forty-niners and other emigrants on their way to California found it a useful place to replenish supplies or make repairs. Army officers, journalists, and politicians all rode in to satisfy their curiosity about the town and the odd marital customs of its residents. Now, with convenient connections from the Union Pacific or Central Pacific to the Utah Central Railroad, it's practically de rigueur for everyone to make the detour. As one chronicler peevishly notes, "A maudlin curiosity induces many travelers to time their arrival at Ogden on Saturday, so that they may branch off and spend Sunday at Salt Lake City, take a drive of an hour or two there, go to the Tabernacle meeting…, peep into some dwelling where a man is supposed to have more than one wife, and return in time to take the Sunday evening train for the West."

Don't be put off by his comments. There's much more than that to see, beginning with the surprising beauty of the landscape as you approach the city. The mountain range to the east forms a wall that glistens with snow much of the year and gleams purple and gray at twilight. To the west lies the body of water that gives the city its name, rippling blue and silver in the sun, and beckoning onlookers to test its fabled buoyancy. As you enter the town itself, you will be surprised at how green it is. In platting their residential neighborhoods, the Mormons have left generous spaces for gardens, small orchards, and shade trees around their houses, and dug irrigation ditches to keep these plots well watered and blooming.

It's all a part of the design for a sublime temple city. The ruler-straight boulevards are 116 feet wide and laid out in an orderly grid from the edges of Temple Square's ten acres: West Temple Street beginning along its western edge; South Temple along the south; and East Temple – now commonly called Main Street – extending down from the eastern edge of the square, where the town's commercial establishments stretch for several long blocks.

There are two fine hotels. The brick Walker House, on Main Street, rises four stories high, affording mountain views from some of its elegantly furnished 132 rooms. Gas lighting in the accommodations? Of course – as well as hot and cold baths, a barbershop, and a billiards salon for the gentlemen. A longtime favorite, the Townsend House on West Temple Street, was sold to new proprietors at the beginning of the year and renamed the Continental, but its 150 rooms remain as lovely as ever, and shaded piazzas still grace the front of the building. You'd be comfortable at either establishment, and only steps away from all the marvels of the City of the Saints.

Where to begin? Well, if you're worn out from your journey, ride the mule-drawn streetcar to the warm sulfur springs for a bit of restorative soaking. Turkish baths, hot-air baths, Russian baths, and natural baths are all available. Just don't linger in the tub too long, or you'll be too limp to sightsee.

The Tabernacle should be first on your list. Its unusual design has been described as resembling "half of a gigantic egg, split lengthwise." Since its completion in 1867, it has hosted thousands of the faithful at their worship services each Sunday and will continue to do so until the Temple, whose elaborate granite structure has been under construction for years, is finished. Till then, you can join the throngs on the Sabbath to listen to the sermon of one of the elders and the sounds of the gigantic organ, fashioned in Salt Lake City and said to be the second largest on the continent.

On South Temple Street, behind a wall, you'll find the residences of the late Brigham Young and his family – or perhaps one should say families, for he led by example and was a much-married man. His Beehive House, built

*" We sallied forth to view the city of the Saints, with the same odd
sort of excitement and vague expectation one must experience
in Constantinople or Tangiers. "*

Mrs. Frank Leslie, *California: A Pleasure Trip*
from Gotham to the Golden Gate, 1877

of adobe like most of Salt Lake City's earliest dwellings, is a grand Greek
Revival home with a two-story veranda and a cupola adorned with a sculpture of a beehive. Here the apostle maintained his own rooms, along with a
nearby office and reception area where he greeted the visitors who streamed
in to meet him. As they departed Brother Brigham usually admonished
them to "print the truth," though writers often interpreted "the truth"
according to their own preconceptions.

Next door is the Lion House, named for the stone animal that crowns
the entryway, perhaps warning prying visitors away. Also built of adobe
blocks, the building is long, with twenty steep gables on the second floor,
each containing a bedroom for one of Young's children and childless wives.
His spouses with offspring had quarters on the first floor, and a number of
the women and children continue to occupy the home. Be sure to look at the
"Amelia Palace" across the way, with its imposing tower, capacious verandas,
and dozens of decorative windows. The dwelling is an architectural homage
to the wife who reportedly held Young's highest regard.

"Smooth, glistening, gray, and of a faultless oval, large enough to shelter 17,000 persons,"
a traveler wrote of the Tabernacle, where Mormons have worshiped since 1867.

" The stores, I may remark, are far superior, in all points, to the shops in an English country town that is not a regular watering-place. "

Richard Burton, *The City of the Saints and Across the Rocky Mountains to California*, 1862

There are many other interesting buildings in the neighborhood. The Tithing Office is where Mormon faithful contribute a tenth of their yearly income – in coin or kind – to the church. The Museum, run by a Professor Barfoot and located just opposite the Tabernacle, displays a fascinating array of natural wonders and local wares, from ore samples and precious desert minerals to Indian pottery and Utah silk, as well as a small collection of birds and reptiles.

And don't miss the Zion's Cooperative Mercantile Institution, better known as the Co-op, whose magnificent cast-iron façade is ornamented in black and gold with the words "Holiness to the Lord." This up-to-date emporium grew out of an attempt to ensure Mormon self-sufficiency in all things. Believers were encouraged to shun all enterprises own by 'Gentiles' (as non-Mormons, including the town's Jewish merchants, were known), though that boycott ended a decade ago.

The city has now begun to erect some distinguished commercial structures downtown. There's the substantial brick Deseret National Bank and William Jennings's Eagle Emporium, which has made him the territory's first millionaire. In front is a favorite local landmark – a four-sided clock powered by a water wheel and originally transported here by ox-drawn wagon.

With its cast-iron architectural sculpture, the façade of the Zion's Cooperative Mercantile Institution is a landmark on Salt Lake City's Main Street.

A SIDE TRIP TO THE GREAT SALT LAKE

Just as its namesake city often evokes comparisons to distant points of the globe, so the Great Salt Lake, a pleasant 18-mile journey from Temple Square, frequently reminds visitors of the Dead Sea of Palestine or some equally exotic place. No less a globetrotter than Richard Burton announced, "we seemed to look upon the sea of the Cyclades."

The body of water is salty indeed: A salt works on the lake produces mounds of the condiment. And though no fish swim in its depths, a profusion of wild fowl hover around the marshes that fringe the shore. Several islands in the lake are even large enough for city folk to graze herds of cattle.

Gather friends, pack a picnic and your bathing costume, and aim for the sandy beach near Black Rock, where a pier extends out from the shore. (Don't worry if you come unprepared; you'll be able to procure snacks and bathing suits on the spot.) Then wade in. You'll find it easy to float. In fact, you'll probably find it difficult not to. Afterwards, be sure to rinse yourself with fresh water from head to toe, lest you return to your hotel with as white a crown as the Wasatch Mountains.

Meanwhile, catering to the needs of Salt Lake City's 20,000 inhabitants are all manner of shops purveying food, drygoods, furnishings, and services, including Savage's Picture Gallery, whose photographic scenes of the town make fine souvenirs.

Providing entertainment – everything from Shakespeare to singers – is the Salt Lake Theatre, with its Greek-inspired façade. And contrary to what you might expect, Salt Lake City is home to two breweries, several saloons, and even a discreet row of houses where men may seek female company.

Events of the day are reported in the daily press, which one popular guidebook advises is "exceedingly peculiar," citing the *Daily News* as the church organ, the *Daily Herald* as the livelier voice of the progressive Mormons, the *Daily Tribune* as the stinging journal of the opposition, and the *Mail* as an evening paper under Gentile influences. It remains true, as Richard Burton observed, "that in Great Salt Lake City there are three distinct opinions concerning, three several reasons for, and three diametrically different accounts of, every thing that happens."

You must come and draw your own conclusions. Or just come and enjoy the scenery. Perhaps some enterprising person will think of a way to turn those snowcapped peaks into a winter playground of Olympian proportions.

THE MORMON TRAIL

How do you reckon the length of the Mormons' journey to their New Jerusalem? It's more than 1,200 miles from their previous headquarters at Nauvoo, Illinois, to Salt Lake City. But the story begins a thousand miles farther east in Fayette, New York, where Joseph Smith had a religious vision in which an angel handed him golden plates. From those he translated the *Book of Mormon*, whose teachings underpinned the Church of Jesus Christ of Latter-Day Saints that he founded in 1830.

Smith and his growing array of followers soon moved to Ohio, then on to Missouri, and in 1839 to Nauvoo, where they built a towering Temple. However, clashes with surrounding communities over Mormon organization and beliefs – including whispers about plural marriage – led to Smith's death in an Illinois jail cell in 1845 and a desire by the rest of the faithful to set up their own independent state.

Led by Brigham Young, the church apostle who took over for Smith, the first pioneers headed west in 1846. Setting up winter quarters on the Missouri River, they dug in for several months. Then the following April, an initial party of 148 moved across the Plains, edging the north bank of the Platte River to Fort Laramie, where they followed the Oregon Trail and crossed the Continental Divide at South Pass. Right in their wake came the main group, pushing over the Wasatch Mountains and down into the Valley of the Great Salt Lake, which Brigham Young entered on July 24, 1847.

Thousands of Mormons, including many immigrants from the British Isles and Scandinavia, would follow in their tracks over the next two decades, riding in wagons or simply pushing handcarts as they made their way on foot to their promised land.

SANTA FE, NEW MEXICO TERRITORY

Can there be a more enchanting town in the West than Santa Fe? Even though a brand-new railroad spur line now deposits you at a depot not far from the Plaza, an atmosphere of long-ago times and faraway places slows the pace of daily life. "A drowsy town," Susan Wallace, the wife of the Territorial Governor, recently called it, with "every requisite of romance, – the enchantment of distance, the charm of the unknown, – and, in shadowy mists of more than three hundred years, imagination may flower out in fancies rich and strange."

Indeed, history is embedded in the very walls of the city. Founded around 1610 by Don Pedro de Peralta, Santa Fe was laid out according to traditional Spanish ordinances, with the Casa Real, the seat of government, along the northern edge of the grassy square that was also the town's religious and mercantile center. From this outpost, Peralta and those who followed him governed a land where Pueblo Indians had dwelled for centuries.

The twisting streets of Santa Fe still reflect the old Spanish town that has stood here for centuries. The steeples of St. Francis Cathedral are merely an artist's imagining of the archbishop's plans.

Peralta's "palace" still stands, though it has been the site of much upheaval. During the Pueblo Revolt of 1680, the Indians attacked the Spanish and drove them out, turning the building into a fortress of their own. A dozen years later, the Spanish regained the upper hand and reestablished their capital on this spot. Today the venerable one-story adobe structure has been prettily stuccoed and etched to suggest stone. The columns of its old *portal*, a covered porch, have been replaced with milled wooden supports, and there's a new balustrade on the roof, which was finally covered with tin to repel the rain. Notwithstanding these changes, you can easily stand here and imagine what it was like half a century ago, after Mexico declared its independence from Spain, and Anglo traders made their way to the end of the perilous Santa Fe Trail.

Cracking their whips and whooping it up to signal their arrival, the drovers would pull up their wagons on the Plaza and settle in to enjoy the pleasures of this Spanish-speaking *villa*. They smiled at the señoritas, stayed at *la fonda* (the inn), gambled at the monte tables, and danced at fandangos held in the *salas* of the town's haciendas. Then they returned to Missouri to load their wagons with new merchandise and set off again.

WHO ARE THE BUFFALO SOLDIERS?

Black troops have served on the frontier for decades as members of the Ninth and Tenth Cavalry and the Twenty-Fourth and Twenty-Fifth Infantry. Their courage during the Civil War led to the organization of their permanent regiments, and some say it was their bravery and strength – like that of the buffalo – that inspired the Indians to give black soldiers their nickname. Others claim it refers to the buffalo robes that are part of these troopers' winter wear, or the resemblance of the soldiers' thick, dark hair to the animal's coat.

Posted first in Texas and Kansas and later in New Mexico, the buffalo soldiers have proudly guarded mail routes, railroad crews, and telegraph lines, patrolled the border, and played a part in the Indian wars throughout the Southwest. At Fort Marcy, the regimental band also entertains in the Plaza, and their rendition of "John Brown's Body" is not soon forgotten.

Wagons make their way past the *portales* lining the south, commercial side of the Plaza, in an illustration showing the *villa* in 1873.

In 1846 the opening salvos of the Mexican–American War had just been fired when Brigadier General Stephen Kearny raised the American flag in the Plaza; two years later Santa Fe was officially U.S. territory. Nevertheless, when you get off the Atchison, Topeka & Santa Fe train, and see the "daughters of New Mexico," as one traveler called them, "unstaycd and unpadded, who have gained nothing from conventionalism, and have grown up to their full estate in blissful ignorance of milliner's modes," you'll know you're not in Kansas anymore.

The *fonda* was rebuilt a decade ago, and today it's the Exchange Hotel, conveniently located at the southeast corner of the Plaza on San Francisco Street. This had always been "the" place to stay – possibly because it was the only one – but it now has competition from the new Palace Hotel a couple of blocks north. You'll recognize that hostelry immediately by its three wooden stories and Second Empire-style mansard roof towering over its low-rise adobe neighbors.

Wherever you decide to sleep, begin your explorations with the Governor's Palace, as the Casa Real is now called. Don't expect Spanish Colonial grandeur. The *New Mexican*, the local paper, has noted that the official residence, which includes the Territorial Library and the Senate Chamber, as well as other offices, is now as "speckled and spotted as Joseph's coat" and overshadowed by more recent two-story buildings around the Plaza.

The shops here cater to your every need: general merchandise at Z. Staab & Co.; liquor, groceries, cigars, clothing, and carpets at Seligman & Clever's, a local fixture for thirty-five years; and the newspaper and post office next to Johnson's drygoods store. The Spiegelberg brothers are busy constructing a grand new store on San Francisco Street, with metal cornices, English tiles, and skylights. You can gauge their progress as you stroll down the avenue toward St. Francis Cathedral.

The church is just one of the projects inaugurated by Archbishop Jean-Baptiste Lamy since he arrived in Santa Fe in 1851. He's an unforgettable character – surely worthy of a novel – and he's putting a twin-towered stone Romanesque house of worship over the simple adobe *parroquia*, the parish church that has stood here since the 1700s. Only a single chapel remains, home to a beloved statue of the Virgin, known as La Conquistadora, that was brought by Spanish soldiers in 1625. Each year, as part of Corpus Christi ceremonies, the statue is paraded through the streets of Santa Fe and then returned to its niche.

A few blocks away on College Street, as the Old Santa Fe Trail is now known, you'll find the Chapel of Our Lady of Light, ordered by Archbishop Lamy for the Sisters of the Order of Loretto. Lamy's stonemasons produced a charming Gothic-style sanctuary but neglected to leave room for a stairway to the choir loft. The problem was solved – some say miraculously – when a carpenter appeared, fashioned an elegant wooden spiral staircase, and disappeared without asking for payment.

If you follow College Street across the Santa Fe River, you'll come to the Barrio de Analco, an artisan and workers' neighborhood little changed from bygone days. Don't be deterred by the woebegone appearance of the San Miguel Mission. Its bell tower may have collapsed, but the simple place of worship has stood here since 1710; you can make out the date on the beam above the choir loft. Inside is an ancient wooden altar screen, set off by religious paintings on deer and buffalo hide and a striking statue of the church's patron saint.

Across the way is the "oldest house," according local lore, though no one truly knows its age. Some say the handmade adobe walls may go back to some long-forgotten Indian pueblo. Other traditional dwellings line atmospheric streets like Canyon Road, where you'll often see woodcutters leading donkeys laden with firewood for sale, a picturesque sight indeed.

"MI CASA ES SU CASA..."

Santa Fe's traditional adobes have a distinctive style, with rooms often arranged end to end, like carriages in a train. Inside, curved fireplaces occupy the corners, and whitewashed walls reach to ceilings supported by log poles called *vigas*, which are covered with *latillas* (smaller sticks), and roofed with mud. Although these houses often present a long wall to the street, punctuated only by small windows and narrow doors, a gracious, shady *placita*, or interior courtyard, awaits you on the other side

If you're curious to see what one of these residences is like, your best opportunity is probably during a fandango. These informal dances take place almost every night, held for feast days or for no reason at all. The furniture in the *sala*, or living room, is moved to one side, and everyone is welcome: mothers and daughters, well-born gallants, and rough workingmen in simple garb. One trader's young wife was fascinated by the scene, including the use of tobacco by women, unheard of in polite Eastern society: "[The ladies] were dressed in the Mexican style; large sleeves, short waists, ruffled skirts, and no bustles...All danced and smoke cigarittos, from the old woman with false hair and teeth... to the little child. 'The Cuna' was danced, and was indeed beautiful; it commences with only two and ends when the floor gets too full for any more to come on."

There's one more church to visit. The Santuario de Guadalupe stands along the old El Camino Real that leads to Mexico City, its adobe bricks topped by a tiered tower with sand-cast copper bells. Inside is an eighteenth-century oil-on-canvas altar screen with a vivid image of the Virgin who lends the chapel its name.

Lest you think Santa Fe has nothing but religious sites to offer the visitor, return across the river to "Burro Alley," where the saloons dispense "Taos lightning," bawdy houses entertain patrons, and card dealers tempt gamblers to try their luck. By day this rowdy precinct is quieter, a better time perhaps to visit Jake Gold's Old Curiosity Shop, where you can buy Pueblo

Adobe dwellings with walled *placitas* line Montoya Hill on the outskirts of Santa Fe. The sun-baked-brick houses often frustrate residents by leaking in the rain.

pottery, Indian blankets, or Spanish carvings to bring home the flavor of Santa Fe. The town's culinary creations are probably more difficult to transport, but at least you can sample the local dishes – *sopas* (soups), *carne de asado* and *carne de cocida* (roasted and boiled meats), flat corn tortillas with which to scoop up *frijoles* (beans), and green and red chile salsas that will dance on your palate.

Take a moment simply to wander the town or find a spot to sit and watch the passing show. As a magazine reporter has noted, "In Santa Fe one may see all classes and conditions of men...Spaniards from El Paso and Chihuahua; blue and gold army officers;...dirt-begrimed bull-whackers, just in from Las Vegas or Arizona; grizzled nervous-looking miners;...troops of slender dark-eyed women," as well as Indians from the pueblos.

Leave some time to climb the hill to Fort Marcy, the star-shaped redoubt constructed by Brigadier General Kearny but never used. He preferred to garrison his men in the former Spanish barracks just north of the Plaza, housing his officers in neat adobe cottages nearby. Today's troops, including the "buffalo soldiers" of the Ninth Cavalry, continue that practice. And unnecessary though it turned out to be, the fort does afford a fine view.

> *"* ...nothing is more general, throughout the country, and with all classes than dancing. From the gravest priest to the buffoon – from the richest nabob to the beggar – from the governor to the ranchero – from the soberest matron to the flippant belle – from the grandest señora to the cocinera – all partake of the exhilarating amusement. *"*

Josiah Gregg, *Commerce of the Prairies*, 1844

There will be music in the air as you return to town for the evening. "It is the friendly custom of citizens of Santa Fe to gather about the Plaza," Mrs. Wallace notes, "with their wives and children, in carriages and in porches, and listen to the music of the military band." Three times a week, the Ninth Cavalry musicians perform in the gaily painted gazebo in the park. "Pretty children in white dresses and gay ribbons play on the sidewalks; gallant horsemen dash before us; and young men and maidens promenade the gravel walks under the cottonwood trees, telling the old, old story, new every morning and fresh every evening." A story as timeless as Santa Fe itself.

THE CREATIVE SPIRIT

Is there something in Santa Fe's adobes that inspires a creative spirit? Perhaps it's in the water of the *acequias*, the traditional irrigation canals that course lazily through town. Certainly Governor Lew Wallace found that his story flowed swiftly from his pen as he finished writing *Ben Hur* late at night in his rain-stained office in the Palace of the Governors. Published just a few months ago, the "first edition of Ben Hur has been exhausted," the *New Mexican* has proclaimed, adding that a second edition is on the way immediately.

For generations the town has been known for its artisans. Skilled silver- and goldsmiths, weavers, and woodcarvers have produced marvelous articles for churches and residences alike. Until now, though, painters have been notably absent. Surely that will soon change as artists discover New Mexico's mesa-and-cactus landscapes, its evocative adobe missions, and its Indian inhabitants' age-old pueblos – scenes to kindle the imagination and fill canvases with color and light.

TOMBSTONE, ARIZONA TERRITORY

There's a tale of good fortune behind the dour name of this rough-and-ready mining town in southern Arizona. In 1877, a bearded prospector named Ed Schieffelin, undaunted by the Apaches who still roamed these parched hills, thought the land looked promising. When he said as much to the cavalrymen at Fort Huachuca, they laughed and told him all he'd find was his tombstone. But Schieffelin proved them wrong. He discovered silver and celebrated by naming his claim Tombstone. The next year he found an even richer vein, and dubbed that mine the Lucky Cuss. Almost instantly, it seemed, the word spread, and ever since then, this once-remote spot a few miles north of Mexico has been swarming with prospectors, suppliers, saloonkeepers, and gamblers eager to share in the wealth.

Visiting Tombstone is an opportunity to watch a town spring up before your very eyes. Just last year, a town plan was imposed on the jumble of land claims, and the makeshift canvas tents are giving way to wooden buildings for stores and houses. Tombstone also offers a chance to rub shoulders with some larger-than-life men you may have heard of. But Ed Schieffelin won't be among them. Someone recently offered him $300,000 for his claims, and he's taken the money and left town.

To get to Tombstone, make your way by railroad to Benson, Arizona, where a stagecoach departs daily. That 31-mile trip will take you six and a half hours, and costs a half-eagle – a $5 gold piece – though sometimes rival coach lines will fight for customers and drive down the price. Find a seat, watch out for the desperadoes who have been known to attack the stage, and hold on to your hat. But pack your guns away in your valise. A recent local ordinance now forbids anyone but lawmen to carry them in town.

As you ride into Tombstone, you'll understand why. The hill just north of town is the newly laid-out cemetery, but in

The *Tombstone Epitaph*, recently established by editor John Clum, has begun to inveigh against cattle rustling by lawless cowboys.

" The camp is considered a remarkably quiet one – only one murder since my arrival. *"*

Clara Brown, *San Diego Union*, July 14, 1880

just a few months it's begun to fill up. Locals call it Boot Hill, because so many of its inhabitants died with their boots on. Like Tom Waters, who got into an altercation in a saloon over remarks about his black-and-blue-checked shirt. Or Mike Killeen, who was killed either by Buckskin Frank Leslie or his friend George Perine – witnesses disagree – over Killeen's estranged wife, May. Leslie has now married the widow. As for live residents, the town currently boasts almost 1,000, with respectable mine officials, lawyers, politicians, and a few wives swelling the ranks of earlier arrivals.

If you come in summer, expect it to be hot, windy, and dusty. But you won't have any trouble slaking your thirst. At last count there were twenty-six saloons (though that number may have increased in the last week), and their swinging doors are open twenty-four hours a day. The Crystal Palace has double gas lamps, patterned wallpaper, and a carved wooden back bar. Similar appointments grace the Alhambra, where the black walnut bar is embossed in gold, and paintings and engravings copied from Old Masters hang on the walls. A three-piece orchestra plays as patrons try their luck at the three gambling tables. The finest of them all is the new Oriental Saloon, "the most elegantly furnished saloon this side of the favored city of the Golden Gate," according to the *Tombstone Epitaph*. It has a carved bar finished in white and gilt, twenty-eight-burner chandeliers, Brussels carpet, and a brace of sideboards originally commissioned for the Baldwin Hotel of San Francisco. Plus it includes the largest gambling setup in town.

There are countless places in Tombstone to wager on faro, keno, or poker, for big stakes or small, but at the Oriental you might find Wyatt Earp (he's said to have an owner's share in the place), his friend Doc Holliday, or even Bat Masterson or Luke Short, who recently arrived from Dodge City to work as dealers.

ABOVE Welcome to Tombstone! Turning out to greet the stagecoach, the town's solid citizens present a united front for a community portrait.

Earp came to town with his brothers last year, and their presence has been noted by every resident of Tombstone. Virgil is now the deputy U.S. marshal here; Morgan is a special deputy and sometime shotgun messenger; James tends bar; and Wyatt has worked as a Wells Fargo guard, but those in the know claim he's about to be named undersheriff for the county. He's promised to do something about the cattle rustling and raids into Mexico that have begun to rouse the concern of federal authorities.

Certainly in daytime you should feel in no danger as you walk the streets of town. It's easy to find your way around this busy, bustling place, though you may have to dodge the carpenters and workmen putting up shops all around you. There are only five main thoroughfares, crossed by numbered streets. The bars, dancehalls, and "female boarding houses" mostly run along Allen Street, and there's a Chinese quarter called Hop Town at the west end of town. Elsewhere, on Fremont or Toughnut Streets and the adjoining blocks you'll encounter all the merchandise and services you might require: tailor; locksmith and gunsmith; hardware and knives; drygoods, clothing, boots, and shoes; mining and milling machinery; a wagon company; a livery stable; and the constantly busy Watt & Tarbell undertakers.

As for places to stay, you have your choice of hotels and boarding houses. There's the Occidental, and the two-story brick Cosmopolitan, which boasts fifty rooms. The Mohave Hotel, one of Tombstone's first, which opened in a tent in 1879, has been reborn as Brown's Hotel in more permanent surroundings. The recently constructed Grand Hotel lives up to its name the minute you walk into the front entrance. A handsome staircase with a black-

COLT .45

They call it the "peacemaker." It's a favorite weapon of local law officers Wyatt Earp and Bat Masterson. The Colt's Manufacturing Company has made its Single Action Army handgun, also known as the Colt .45, since 1873, and it's been popular throughout the West ever since. Price? Just $12 for a standard six-shooter, though you can order the barrel to different lengths and with specially detailed handles.

The single action means you have to fully cock the hammer each time before you pull the trigger. If you use your thumb, you'll understand why they call this method the "thumb buster." For quick firing, some gunfighters hold down the trigger with the right hand and "fan" the hammer with the left. It may not be the most accurate way to fire, but at close range the black powder cartridge will still do serious damage. Whatever you do, the code of the West is clear: Don't draw your gun in any argument unless you intend to use it.

RIGHT The gun that won the West: The standard Cavalry Colt .45 comes with a 7½-inch barrel; shorter versions are known as "Civilian" or "Gunfighter" models.

walnut banister leads to the main hall, where the beautifully furnished bridal chamber awaits the next happy couple.

These establishments all tout their fine dining rooms, and the Rockaway Oyster House also has its adherents. But take special note of The Russ House, a hotel and restaurant newly under the management of Miss Nellie Cashman, a native of Ireland who began cooking in the mining camps of Nevada, ran a boarding house in British Columbia, and made a fine reputation for herself as the owner of the Delmonico Restaurant in Tucson. She serves memorable dinners for 50 cents a meal.

Much simpler is the boarding house run by Camillus and Mollie Fly on Fremont Street, next to a yard of the O.K. Corral. The accommodations are less noteworthy than the photographic studio the couple maintains next door. Camillus is a noted artist with the camera lens and a leading frontier photojournalist. Take the time to sit for a portrait and have your visit to Tombstone immortalized.

The events of the day are covered by two newspapers: the Democrat-leaning *Nugget*, which has existed for a couple of years, and the Republican *Epitaph*, the few-months-old creation of the talented John Clum. His experience as an Indian agent gives him a unique perspective on relations with the Apaches, who sometimes still menace the area. But he also assiduously covers everything from new businesses to political developments and courtroom trials.

Meanwhile, there's the excitement of additional entertainments on the horizon. Al Schieffelin, the brother of Tombstone's founding miner, is building an opera house that will welcome the finest performers in America. And the Birdcage is about to open with a small theater, as well as a saloon and gambling rooms. The owner has ordered an elaborate bar shipped around Cape Horn, as well as a grand piano to accompany singers on the stage. He also promises an interior unlike any seen before, with curtained cages – like little gilded birdcages – for his delicate (if somewhat soiled) doves to entertain their gentlemen friends. Perhaps someone will write a song about them.

Much fame awaits Tombstone. Town boosters say with confidence that from now on, everything will be O.K.!

VIRGINIA CITY, NEVADA

You'll ride into town aboard the Virginia & Truckee Railroad – the V & T – which chugs its winding way from Carson City. Don't expect a fast trip; there are many twists, curves, and turns as the train works its way uphill through a treeless landscape of hills and canyons, past the neighboring community of Gold Hill, and then a final two miles to Virginia City itself, the boisterous site of the Big Bonanza, on Nevada's legendary Comstock Lode.

The fabled "Queen of the Comstock" is now home to perhaps 20,000 souls, including some of the millionaires who made their fortunes here. But Virginia City is still an industrial place, with chimneys of mine buildings

Frank Leslie's Illustrated Newspaper shows Virginia City's animated C Street in 1877, rebuilt after a fire, its high style befitting the wealthy metropolis of 20,000 souls.

MINING THE COMSTOCK

The very size of the Comstock Lode posed problems for the companies that tried to mine it. At 50 feet down, the vein was more than 10 feet wide in places; at 150 feet the silver might actually extend in a 40- or 50-foot swath. How could one excavate it without the earth collapsing? Compounding the problem, the wet, claylike soil of the area was unstable, so conventional timbers couldn't hold up the tunnels.

A German-born engineer named Philipp Deidesheimer came up with an answer: He had lumber cut into 18-by-18-inch supports that were 6 or 7 feet tall. Across the top – and interlocked into them – were 5-foot-long braces. This technique, called square-set timbering, created extremely strong cells that could be constructed in any space and extended as the miners cleared rock. Deidesheimer's innovation is now being used throughout the West.

The only thing needed is wood, lots of it, from the forests of the Sierra Nevada. It hasn't taken long for the green slopes surrounding blue Lake Tahoe to be stripped bare to shore up Virginia City's mines.

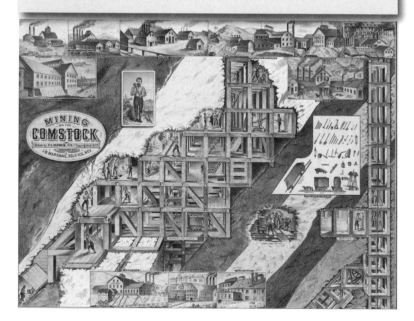

EVERY MAN JACK

Virginia City is home to many nationalities, but Cornishmen, famed for their mining skills, are among the most numerous immigrants working on the Comstock Lode. They're often called "Cousin Jacks," thanks to their habit of bringing along a fellow countryman when a job is in the offing and introducing him as "my Cousin Jack."

That nickname accounts for some other mine vocabulary. A hand-held rock drill is known as a "jack hammer," while drilling holes alone is "single jacking," as opposed to "double jacking," or working in pairs.

The Cornishmen have also imported their belief in mining elves. The "tommyknockers" are said to rap on underground timbers to warn of hazards, punish greedy miners, and occasionally bestow a lucrative discovery on some lucky Jack.

and ore processors bristling all around, and piles of tailings marking the entrances to shafts, like piles of dirt at a gopher hole. No matter what time you step off the train, the streets are likely to be noisy with the sounds of hoisting works and stamping mills, as the mine shifts work around the clock.

Still, this is hardly the rude mining camp described by *Harper's Weekly* correspondent J. Ross Browne two decades ago, in his "Peep at Washoe" – as miners called what was then part of Utah Territory – where he found "frame shanties, pitched together as if by accident, tents of canvas, of blankets, of brush, of potato-sacks and old shirts, with empty whisky-barrels for chimneys; smoky hovels of mud and stone...." Shortly before Browne's visit, the prospectors who lived in these shacks had realized that the dark blue mud that clogged their diggings was actually silver of the highest grade!

One of those first miners, James "Old Virginny" Finney, is said to have named the town after his home state, christening it with what was left in his

OPPOSITE A cross-section of the Belcher Mine reveals its up-to-date equipment and mining technology, including the square-set timbering that makes it possible to extract the silver of the Comstock Lode.

bottle after a toot. The name of the Comstock Lode came about after Henry P. Comstock blustered his way into a share of a lucrative claim worked by two Irish fortune seekers. Most of the characters from those rougher times have now sold out and moved on; the mining today is the province of big companies who can finance the elaborate works necessary to reach the veins of ore and then process the silver – millions and millions of dollars' worth.

There have been some bumps along the way. After the initial boom (which was lucrative enough to make Nevada its own territory and then a state), and many gyrations in the price of mine stock, the ore began to dwindle. Then, in 1873, just as it seemed Virginia City might fade like so many other mining camps, the company owned by John Mackay, James Fair, James Flood, and William O'Brien found the Big Bonanza, and with that unbelievably rich lode, the town has flourished anew.

On October 26, 1875, a devastating fire swept through the center of town, obliterating not only old wooden buildings but also those of brick. Still, as one resident put it, "The people of the Comstock are no drones." Within six months Virginia City's homes and business had been reconstructed, and the town is now even grander than before.

With its alphabetical streets terraced into the slope of Mount Davidson, the metropolis is easy to navigate. You can walk along A Street, for instance, and look down on the roofs of B, and so on. The finest place to stay is the International Hotel, newly rebuilt between C and B Streets. You can't miss it. The brick hotel stands six stories high, with an elevator to whisk you up to your spotless accommodations. The public rooms gleam with fine mahogany furniture, ceiling-high mirrors, and magnificent chandeliers, and the dining room and saloon are known as meeting places for local politicians and mine owners. If you prefer something away from the spotlight, you'll be quite comfortable at the Frederick House or the Molinelli Hotel only a few doors away.

B Street also boasts the new Storey County Courthouse, whose cupola tops a ornate cream-and-white façade on which a statue of Justice weighs her scales without anything over her eyes. It seems Justice is not blind in Virginia City!

Down the hill, on E Street, you'll notice the red-and-white steeple of St. Mary's in the Mountains. Though badly damaged in the fire, the so-called Bonanza Church has risen again with the support of John Mackay's millions, and the bell and pewter baptismal font from the earlier sanctuary have been reinstalled. You can join the crowds in the carved wooden pews beneath soaring Gothic redwood arches and hear Father Patrick Manogue say Mass.

Other religious denominations are well represented in Virginia City – not surprising in a town that's home to immigrants from every corner of Europe, as well as Hispanic, Indian, black, and Chinese inhabitants. The Baptists and Presbyterians face off on C Street, while the Episcopalians and Methodists have their own churches, and the Jewish residents worship at a synagogue in the north end of the city.

C Street, the main business thoroughfare, is lined by one- and two-story structures with balconies that shade the sidewalk. The avenue bustles with banks and telegraph offices, the Wells Fargo Express Office, stationery and

BREEZES AND BURROS

Almost every visitor to Virginia City remarks on the gales that threaten to spirit them away. According to reporter Dan DeQuille, Washoe "zephyrs" can "snatch a man's hat off his head and take it vertically a hundred feet into the air."

Since DeQuille is famous for his observations of natural phenomena, who would doubt his story that "in the spring of 1863, a donkey was caught up from the side of Mount Davidson…and carried eastward over the city, at a height of 500 or 600 feet above the houses, finally landing near the Sugar-Loaf Mountain – nearly 5 miles away."

Speaking of donkeys, DeQuille solemnly opines that these "Washoe canaries" (named for their warbling hee-haw) "swalloweth woolen shirts, old breeches, gunny sacks and dilapidated hoop-skirts when in a state of pensive good nature – what, then must we suppose hym capable of swallowing, once hys wrath is enkindled?"

" Board at. . .the first-class restaurant is \$1 a day, or 'four bits' a meal; but you will get everything that the market affords and the market of Virginia City affords everything that grows which is fit to eat, and a thousand and one things which are not fit to eat. "

Mary McNair Mathews, *Ten Years in Nevada*, 1880

bookstores, grocery stores, mercantiles, the National Guard Hall, fine restaurants, and, of course, saloons. *The Territorial Enterprise*, the lively morning newspaper, maintains its offices here, with Dan DeQuille (real name William Wright) reporting the news – or perhaps ornamenting it a bit. Virginia City has been lucky in its fourth estate: *The Enterprise*, the *Evening Chronicle*, and the *Gold Hill Daily News* have employed keen critics of political shenanigans, as well as imaginative wordsmiths.

Among DeQuille's colleagues was young Samuel Clemens, who took his now-famous pen name in Virginia City. Although midwesterners claim that the nom de plume was inspired by the customary shout of the riverboat captains on the Mississippi, locals insist that it came from the writer's habit of stopping by Piper's Corner Saloon, ordering a drink for himself and a fellow journalist, and asking that the bill be chalked up on the board ("mark twain"). In any case, Mr. Twain, who has since returned to the East Coast, put Virginia City on the map when he published his adventures in *Roughing It*, just eight years ago.

Hotel splendor reaches its peak in the fashionable International Hotel, with a saloon that's a meeting place for Virginia City's movers and shakers.

" Virginia was a busy city of streets and houses above ground. Under it was another busy city, down in the bowels of the earth, where a great population of men thronged in and out among an intricate maze of tunnels and drifts…and over their heads towered a vast web of inter-locking timbers that held the walls of the gutted Comstock apart. "

Mark Twain, *Roughing It*, 1872

At the end of C Street is the Fourth Ward School, "the pride of Virginia," as *The Enterprise* called it when it opened in 1876. It's a model of wooden construction with three stories and a basement beneath the fine mansard roof. The sixteen high-ceilinged classrooms accommodate more than a thousand students at individual desks.

Take the time to stroll along Millionaire's Row on B Street, where one of the mine superintendents has modeled his residence on a French castle. Henry Piper, who runs the opera house and saloon with his brother John, recently built a well-appointed two-story home with a pretty bay window, and on A Street there are several new Italianate mansions.

The Chollar Mine's superintendent lives and works in the gracious home where he wined and dined President Grant last year. And John Mackay has taken over the dwelling built by George Hearst to double as the office for the Gould and Curry Mine. Hearst cashed out his Virginia City investments some time ago; meanwhile Mackay has added his own touches to the décor, notably a dining-room chandelier made of silver from his mines. He frequently dines alone, however, as his wife spends much of her time conducting salons in New York and Paris.

When you're ready for dinner, you'll have a choice of two dozen restaurants. Everyone dines out in Virginia City, and the menus are elaborate. The Chauval French Restaurant features antelope steaks and entrees from Delmonico's; others offer oyster appetizers, exotic fruits and ices, delectable pastries and cakes, and champagne. Don't assume your fellow diners will be in last year's garb. Dressmakers and milliners here re-create the latest fashions for the ladies, while haberdashery shops outfit their husbands.

Be sure to stop in at Piper's Opera House, where Shakespeare, melodramas, vaudeville, lectures, boxing matches, and dances are offered almost every day. Seats in the U-shaped gallery cost just 50 cents, proscenium boxes close to the raked stage $15. On rare nights when the theater is dark, try the Masonic or Odd Fellows Halls. And the Temperance Society often hosts speakers in their lodge. That group has its work cut out for it: Some say Virginia City boasts as many as 100 watering holes, which cater to every class of customer, along with countless billiard halls and gambling dens to tempt the gentlemen.

The privileged may be admitted into the members-only Washoe Club. Besides an opulent saloon on the ground floor, the club has a library, billiard room, dining room, and lounge for cards and conversation upstairs. Other well-known bars include the Delta, the Palace, the El Dorado, and the Sazerac, but there's no shortage of other possibilities, both "bit houses" where the drinks cost just twelve and a half cents, and nicer "two-bit" thirst parlors. The Boston Saloon, owned by one of the town's black citizens, is sociably upscale, while the Hibernia Brewery serves ale, beer, whiskey, and other drinks to a mainly Irish clientele.

Seamier spots with other entertainments are mostly clustered around D Street. Locals still talk about a notorious incident that occurred in that infamous district in 1867. Julia Bulette, a local prostitute and honorary member of one of the fire engine companies – was robbed of her jewels and furs and strangled by John Millain, who paid for the crime with his life.

There is one "underworld" no Virginia City visitor should miss: a journey into one of the shafts, where the miners – mostly Cornishmen – toil to extract the ore that has made this town famous. Your guide will dress you in overalls, a woolen shirt, boots, and a hat, hand you a candle, and lower you in a cage hundreds of feet below the surface. It's hot as Hades, with narrow tunnels, shored up by timbers, that extend in every direction, and vast deafening spaces where men use hammers, drills, picks, and explosives to wrest the metal from the earth and load it onto carts that rumble through the tunnels.

They say that the mines are slowing down and the bonanza may soon peter out again. For the moment, though, everything that glitters in Virginia City is silver.

YELLOWSTONE NATIONAL PARK

" One would scarcely suppose that a mud spring could present us with any beauty; yet, standing on the brim of the crater of one, we must concede that even mud may assume forms which render it attractive. "

Albert Peale, *Philadelphia Press*, 1871

They call it "Wonderland" for a reason. As in Alice's journey through her outlandish realm, the first American national park will amaze you with sights that only get curiouser and curiouser. But Yellowstone is a very real place.

For the moment it's a place for travelers who are willing to trade creature comforts for a glimpse of awe-inspiring wilderness. Until the Northern Pacific Railway rolls its track into Montana – surely just two or three years from now – you'll find yourself on a train to the last station on the NPR or a spur line from Ogden on the transcontinental route. When you get off, you'll board a stagecoach bound for a town where you can hire the "outfit" to bring you into Wonderland. Most visitors choose Bozeman, Livingston, or Virginia City, Montana.

Yes, it's a long, dusty ride. But think of the adventure! Newspaper editors thought the first accounts of travels through Yellowstone unreliable fantasies and were reluctant to publish them. But about a decade ago, forays by respected gentlemen left no doubt that the waterfalls, hot springs, and geysers were real. Perhaps you read Nathaniel Langford's tantalizing stories in *Scribner's Monthly* (or heard one of his lectures), describing how he and his companions came on the great falls of the Yellowstone River in "a gorge through volcanic rocks 50 miles long, and varying from 1,000 to nearly 5,000 feet in depth." He has told of the excitement of watching a geyser spout columns of boiling water more than a hundred feet into the air at regular intervals. "We gave it the name of 'Old Faithful,'" he declared. A year or so later, an official survey brought along photographer William Henry Jackson and artist Thomas Moran. Their images, along with the survey reports, quickly galvanized Congress into creating a national park in 1872.

ONCE UPON A TIME...

Since the days of the fur trappers, men have traded tall tales about Yellowstone. Perhaps the steamy geysers contributed to a lot of hot air. Whatever the reason, wild sagas abound.

Some of the yarns go back to Jim Bridger, they say, a mountain man who traveled here since the 1820s and who was known to stretch the truth in the service of a good story. He is said to have recounted the legend of a mountain made of solid glass – a quality that became obvious only after he took aim at an elk on the other side and his bullet bounced back.

Another story concerned a petrified forest, in which the leaves and branches of the trees were in perfect condition but completely made of stone. Even more astounding, the rabbits, sage hens, the birds in the trees were all in their normal places, but as petrified as the forest itself.

Almost every park visitor has been entertained by hearing how anglers would fish in Yellowstone Lake, reel in their catches, and flick them into a nearby hot spring to be cooked up for dinner.

Is it true? Does it matter? What could be more unbelievable than the actual marvels of Yellowstone?

Hoteliers have been slow to ask for the opportunity to create park facilities. At Mammoth Hot Springs, there is a small inn – which one traveler called a "little shanty which is dignified by the name of hotel." At Lower Geyser Basin, an entrepreneur named George Marshall is completing a small log hotel and has just inaugurated a stage line that will carry tourists around the park. For the moment, though, it's far more gratifying to hire your own outfit. Usually, for about $18 a day – count on at least six days for a looping route – you'll get tents, camping equipment, horses, and a wagon, as well as a cook and driver–guide who will ensure that you see the marvels of the area.

Rest assured that travel through Yellowstone has become far safer and easier than it was in the last decade. It's hard to forget the travails of Truman Everts, who wrote about his "Thirty Seven Days of Peril" after he was separated from his friends, including Nathanial Langford, in 1870. When his horse ran off, the intrepid Everts had only the clothes on his back, a couple of knives, and a small opera glass (whose lens he used to produce fire) with which to survive. He lived mostly on thistle roots, growing weaker and more emaciated as he wandered in the wilderness until a search party found him.

Just three years ago, when the U.S. Army pursued Chief Joseph and the Nez Perce through the West, in an attempt to force the last bands of the tribe onto a reservation, the Indians rode through the park and encountered several groups of tourists. To get supplies, the Nez Perce took some of the visitors as hostages, leaving one for dead. At another spot in the park, young warriors shot two other men in retaliation for an earlier battle. After three weeks in Yellowstone, the Nez Perce continued their flight northward, until the Army caught up with them 40 miles from Canada, where Chief Joseph surrendered.

Today Indians no longer threaten Yellowstone tourists. And the park's superintendent, Philetus W. Norris, has lessened your chances of getting lost by erecting guideposts to the trails and putting up signs identifying the principal sights. He has also embarked on a program of connecting the scenic spots by road, though hasty crews have left more than a few tree stumps, which make the way bumpy going. What are a few bumps, though, compared to the glories of Wonderland?

Most tourists will start at Mammoth Hot Springs, where basins of thermally heated water overflow to form spectacular mineralized terraces, delicately tinted by bacteria and algae that vary according to water temperature. The springs gush at unpredictable intervals, forming new terraces, leaving old ones to weather and crumble. In this area you'll see Liberty Cap, named for the old cone's resemblance to French Revolutionary headgear, as well as the dark formation known as Devil's Thumb.

The owner of the rudimentary hotel has also built bathhouses, where you can soak in the mineral hot springs, which many believe are as beneficial to one's health as the fabled spas of Europe. You may wish to leave a small object – a twig or tiny basket, say – with a concessionaire, who will soak it in

" One gentleman tried boiling his dinner in a geyser-spring, but a sudden eruption foiled his plans, blasted his hopes, leaving him dinnerless and disgusted with the business. "

Edwin J. Stanley, *Rambles in Wonderland*, 1878

ABOVE The Fan Geyser lets loose in Midway Geyser Basin, just one of Yellowstone's wondrous thermal areas. Nearby are bubbling mud pots and the famous Old Faithful.

the springs for a few days or overnight and return it to you enveloped in a mineral coating of its own as a souvenir of your experience.

The trail south leads you past the dramatic volcanic glass Obsidian Cliff to the first amazing geysers at Norris Geyser Basin. These may be the hottest and most active group in the park, erupting at unpredictable intervals, with new hot springs bubbling up literally overnight. Take your time to marvel at the sights, but remember that this is just the beginning.

Continue southward, past Gibbon Falls, and toward the Firehole River, which flows toward the three geyser basins of world renown, beginning with the Lower Geyser Basin, where the spouting waters are deep, colorful, and clear. Here the Fountain Paint Pots are filled with hot bubbling mud of various hues, and not far away is the Great Fountain Geyser. At Midway Geyser Basin – known as "Hell's Half Acre" – even more delights await you, including the limpid blue Morning Glory Pool and the ruined battlements and turrets that distinguish Castle Geyser. A few visitors claim to have seen a monstrously large geyser called Excelsior, which erupts rarely but reaches 300 feet high and 300 feet wide when it chooses to show itself.

ABOVE Twenty miles long, and 14 miles wide, Yellowstone Lake exudes serenity and invites a moment of reflection. The lake is home to an abundance of trout, and animals and wildfowl come here to feed. For humans, the lake sunsets nourish the soul.

THE ANIMAL KINGDOM

Hunters have always roamed the Yellowstone region – from Indians who sought food and supplies to fur trappers eager for fine pelts to sell. Early park visitors hunted for sustenance as well as trophies. Thanks to them, in just the last few years, the abundance of animals has been noticeably depleted.

Even so, you're still likely to see an astonishing array of wildlife. Be on the lookout for wolves and coyotes, mule deer, elk, moose, bighorn sheep and pronghorn, as well as ground squirrels, marmots, and tiny pikas. You're more likely to hear a mountain lion than see one, but they're here. Yellowstone is also the realm of Ursus, both smallish black bears and fearsome grizzlies. If you're lucky you may see a bison, though the herds have dwindled.

As for winged creatures, graceful trumpeter swans, sand-hill cranes, herons, pelicans, green-winged teal, and majestic osprey fill the skies.

RIGHT The moose is the largest member of the deer family, often browsing in the marshes at lake's edge.

The overwhelming power and beauty of the Yellowstone's Upper Falls come alive in Thomas Moran's engraving made on his travels with the 1871 Hayden Expedition. The artist added a spectator on the rock in the foreground to give a sense of the size of the cascade.

Throughout the park you're sure to spot wildlife, from bears and elk to countless varieties of birds, though hunters in the past few years seem to have taken more than their share. It's not unlawful to hunt or fish here, but a little restraint will leave enough animals to amaze future visitors, too.

Keep an eye out as well for Superintendent Norris himself, an easily recognizable figure with his long white beard and his usual buckskin garb. He's known to travel frequently through the park – detractors claim in order to affix his name to every stone and tree – but he's a knowledgeable source of information about the region, and he loves to talk.

At last you come to the Upper Geyser Basin and the name that is surely on everyone's lips: Old Faithful. The geyser "well deserves its name," one early visitor observed, "for it spouts with great regularity every hour...seemingly without effort, making no noise." It is a beautiful sight: Rainbows play in the column of water, and the falling spray resembles a shower of diamonds and precious gems. But don't miss the neighboring geysers dotting the bizarre surrounding landscape. Look for the narrow cone of the Beehive and the fountain-like bursts of the Giantess. The well-named Giant spurts a column of water and steam to 250 feet, while the Fan and Mortar geysers sometimes put on their shows at the same time. Finally there is the Grotto, with its spookily white-encrusted cone.

Please resist the example of many tourists who have preceded you and attempted "experiments" in the geyser basin. In days gone by visitors tried to stop the eruptions by tossing in objects – from clothes to cutlery – only to have them spewed out again. Surely this could damage the underground thermal action, and in any case, it's hardly an effective way to do laundry or clean up after a camping dinner.

Tempting as it may be to spend your entire time in Yellowstone camped in this area, you must move on. Follow the trail east past little Mary Lake to the Hayden Valley, then south to the shores of Yellowstone Lake, which is shaped roughly like a hand, albeit with abruptly shortened first and second fingers! There are hot springs and geysers here as well, but the tranquil beauty of the lake itself is charming enough. Savor the play of light on water, and give yourself to the beauty of sunset in the wilderness. This is a respite for the drama still to come.

From here the trail leads back north, to the Mud Geyser that has coated trees with its muck, the awful artillery sounds of the Mud Volcano, and the sizzling tongue of hot water that belches forth from the Dragon's Mouth. You'll cross the astringent waters of Alum Creek and arrive at last at the spot that has inspired brilliant artists and left even great writers at a loss for words.

The Grand Canyon of the Yellowstone River unwinds in two magnificent cascades through a narrow gorge that bursts with color, ranging from the lemon hue that gives the river its name to mossy greens and flaming crimson. It's soul-stirring and unforgettable, a fitting culmination to the sights of the park. From here most visitors will return to Norris Geyer Basin and retrace their route back to Mammoth Hot Springs.

If you have another day or so, however, have your guide take you on to Mount Washburn, whose peak reaches more than 10,000 feet. Those who make the climb will be rewarded with an unparalleled view, as well as the chance to leave their cards in a little metal box that contains those of explorers who have preceded you.

And well you will deserve their company. For in days to come, when a steady stream of tourists pours in by rail and wagon merely to watch Old Faithful erupt, you'll be able to say: I was a traveler to Yellowstone before the crowds came.

YOSEMITE VALLEY, CALIFORNIA

" The face of El Capitan laughed in the moonlight, and the waters of the Yosemite sparkled with silver up and down its whole two thousand feet.**"**

Isaac Bromley, *Scribner's Monthly*, 1872

Who has not yet heard of the great sights of Yosemite? For thirty-five years now, the dramatic valley – and its nearby grove of gargantuan trees – has been extolled, photographed, painted, analyzed, and occasionally derided by countless travelers who have braved a journey into the wilds of California's Sierra Nevada mountains.

James M. Hutchings, one of the earliest to tour the area in 1855, claims to have been rendered speechless at his first encounter. "The truth is, the first view of this convulsion-rent valley, with its perpendicular mountain cliffs, deep gorges, and awful chasms, spread out before us like a mysterious scroll, takes away the power of thinking, much less of clothing thoughts with suitable language." Happily, he brought a photographer on his expedition. Of course, Hutchings soon recovered his powers of description and began to publish his observations in his *Illustrated California Magazine*, which convinced others to follow in his footsteps.

Among the first was a New England clergyman, Rev. Thomas Starr King, whose letters to the *Boston Evening Transcript* in 1860 compared the trail through the valley to the sublime harmonies of Beethoven, proclaiming, "the ninth Symphony is the Yo-Semite of music." He was bowled over by Bridal Veil Fall, with its "ever-melting and renewing tracery" and its "leaping mists and flying shreds." And he paid homage to the "cliff called El Capitan," declaring, "A more majestic object than this rock I expect never to see on this planet. Great is granite, and the Yo-Semite is its prophet!"

With reports like that, it's hardly a surprise that President Lincoln signed a proclamation granting Yosemite Valley and the Mariposa Big Tree Grove

OPPOSITE The granite monolith El Capitan, called Tutokanula by the Indians, epitomizes Yosemite's memorable rocky sights.

" Provide yourselves with good, plain, weather-proof clothes and boots; put money in your purse, and a cheerful and unexacting spirit in your temper . . . and then go your way, prepared to spend a week, if possible, in this wonderful place, whose remembrance will be a delight to you as long as you live. *"*

Mrs. Frank Leslie, *California: A Pleasure Trip from Gotham to the Golden Gate*, 1877

to the state of California as a public trust. And indeed the public has embraced it, making the trek by train, stagecoach, and horseback in ever-increasing numbers. Last year there were actually 1,385 visitors!

Thanks to its popularity, the journey has become less onerous, though you'll still need a taste for adventure and perhaps a sense of humor truly to enjoy Yosemite. These days you can ride a train to Copperopolis, Madera, Modesto, or Merced and board a stagecoach for the rest of the trip. Granted, the ride may be a bit dusty – one traveler claimed there was nothing to do

ABOVE Carleton Watkins demonstrates why Mirror Lake got its name. The photographer's iconic images of Yosemite are a favorite souvenir for visitors.

OPPOSITE In Mariposa Grove, the "Twins" are notable examples of the heights – and forms – that *Sequoia gigantea* can achieve.

WHAT'S IN A NAME?

White men first saw Yosemite in 1851, when a group of soldiers of the Mariposa Battalion pursued a band of Indian raiders into the valley. Over the next few years the Indians, who called themselves the Ahwahneechee and the steep-walled valley Ahwahnee, were virtually routed from the area, with many killed and almost all the rest displaced. A few members of the tribe have returned, however, and live and work around the hotels and camps. Their names for Yosemite's natural monuments adds to the valley's mystery and allure:

Tutokanula – El Capitan

Cholock – Yosemite Fall

Pohono – Bridal Veil Fall

Loya – Sentinel Rock

Tissaack – Half Dome

Piwyack – Vernal Fall

Yowiwe – Nevada Fall

Waiack – Mirror Lake

with the cloud of dust but "chew it and sneeze and try to get used to it" – but at least you no longer have to face a long journey on horseback. The most picturesque itinerary is undoubtedly the Mariposa Route, which deposits you at the Wawona Hotel, just five miles from the "vegetable titans," as Starr King called the giant redwoods. The site has been a resting point for travelers ever since a sickly carpenter named Galen Clark arrived for his health in 1857 and

built a simple mountain cabin. His lodgings grew into a stagecoach stop, and the hospitable Clark, now recovered and a fount of local lore, was eventually named Guardian of Yosemite. The new park commissioners have recently replaced him with James Hutchings, but you may still find Clark guiding one of your expeditions.

Clark's station is now in the hands of the Washburn brothers,

A NOTE TO THE FAIR SEX

No woman should fear a journey to Yosemite. Sally Dutcher made her way to the very summit of Half Dome, guided by George Anderson just a few months after he pioneered the route. The Misses Harriet Kirtland and Anna Park, two schoolteachers from San Francisco, actually camped out in the valley in 1857. Their intrepid spirit has encouraged many of the fair sex to follow, even in the face of long days in the saddle.

And *not* a sidesaddle, one must emphasize. Women travelers here have to ride astride, so they should equip themselves with a Yosemite suit – with a skirt that buttons back to form a kind of bloomer. It's easily purchased in San Francisco, but not everyone finds the garment attractive. Olive Logan, who wrote about her travels for *The Galaxy* magazine, declared: "pardon me once more if I shrink from the task of describing it. It was simply hideous."

Miss Logan is only one of the ladies who have recorded their impressions of Yosemite. Theresa Yelverton, the Viscountess Avonmore, spent several months in the valley and couched her memoir in the form of a novel, *Zanita: A Tale of the Yo-Semite*. The artist Constance Gordon-Cumming immortalized her visit in watercolor and drawings.

For forward-thinking women, the trip to Yosemite may take on greater significance. Only a few years ago, Elizabeth Cady Stanton and Susan B. Anthony donned Yosemite suits and made the excursion during a California tour to promote women's suffrage.

ABOVE Visitors often mount a horse to get closer to the lakes, rocks, and cascades that make the park a "must-see."

OPPOSITE A stagecoach full of tourists winds its way towards Yosemite.

who just last year put up a grand new building. Presidents Ulysses S. Grant and Rutherford B. Hayes are two of the noted guests who have signed the rooms register. But the real celebrities are a short ride away: the towering *Sequoia gigantea* in the grove, including some standouts labeled "Lincoln," "Grant," "Sherman," the "Fallen Monarch," and, at ninety-three feet in circumference, the "Grizzly Giant."

You can spend a comfortable night at Wawona, then rise early to board the stage that crosses a covered bridge and heads for the valley itself. Your first sight of Yosemite, at Inspiration Point, will take your breath away and hint, like the contents page of a book, at the wonders before you: the gray-blue color of the sharp cliff walls, a full stream coursing through a meadow at the bottom, the sounds of a cascade rushing over a precipice. There's nothing to do but climb back into the coach and hold on as it makes its switchback descent some 3,000 feet.

When you reach the valley floor, the sights you've just marveled at from above loom over you, looking even more magnificent. El Capitan's flat granite monolith changes color according to the light, appearing almost ebony in morning shadow, a deceptively soft pink at sunset. Opposite, guarded by Cathedral Rocks, is Bridal Veil Fall, wreathed by rainbows as its billowy flow of water is tossed by the winds.

The valley floor is watered by the Merced River, which is banked by verdant meadows and shaded by oak and sugar pines. Sentinel Rock rakes the sky on one side, while in the distance Half Dome dominates the view of the Upper Valley. Marveling at the bald surface of this mountainous outcrop,

A TRIP THROUGH GOLD COUNTRY

Sonora, Angels Camp, Murphy's, Big Oak Flat, Columbia. Today these California towns are stopping points on the way to Yosemite's treasures. But just three decades ago, they were thronged with fortune seekers who were chasing dreams of different riches. Within months of James Marshall's discovery of a shiny nugget at Sutter's Fort on January 24, 1848, the cry had spread like wildfire in a dry Sierra forest: "Gold…gold from the American River." Shops, ships, and forts were abandoned as men joined the Gold Rush.

By the next summer, mining camps had sprung up everywhere in the foothills, as first a few men found rude shelter on the banks of creeks, then hundreds more put up tents or nailed together makeshift shacks. The so-called Argonauts came from all over the world, clustering in settlements like Chinese Camp and Italian Bar that betrayed their founders' origins. And while these forty-niners panned for "color," the entrepreneurs were moving in, bringing supplies, whiskey, and women.

After the easy pickings were gone from rivers and streams, the miners devised sluices and rockers to separate the gold, and when those no longer sufficed, they built flumes and hydraulic hoses to wear down entire hillsides and uncover the ore.

Some of their camps eventually settled into respectable towns, with churches, opera houses, schools, and general stores that served newly arrived families, even as financiers formed mining companies that could conjure up the funds to sink deeper, more productive shafts. In other places the gold simply played out, the wooden shacks burned, and the prospectors drifted away, until all that was left was the whisper of ghosts and the legends of fortunes made and lost.

you may find it hard to believe that just five years ago George Anderson, a valley settler, conquered its summit by drilling spikes into the rock to hold a rope that aided his ascent.

Soon you'll hear the unmistakable thunder of Yosemite Falls as it cascades almost 2,425 feet in three magnificent tiers. Its music will envelop you during your stay in Yosemite.

And indeed, where *will* you stay? Most visitors seek a room at Barnard's Yosemite Falls Hotel, a complex of buildings that includes the old hand-hewn Cedar Cottage, one of the valley's earliest hostelries. James Hutchings, who ran the hotel under his name in the 1860s, added the Rock Cottage, Oak Cottage, and  River Cottage and even built a parlor around a living tree, though his lodgers in the early days slept in rooms divided only by cloth partitions, with sheets for doors. As for meals, one guest reported, "Sometimes sugar is handed you instead of salt for the trout, or cold water is poured into your coffee." Occasionally knives and forks were forgotten, too, though Hutchings's enthusiasm for the setting often made his visitors forget more practical considerations.

In any case, more substantial, though still rustic, lodgings have now been added, with more conventional dinners on hand. For hygiene and relaxation, Smith's Cosmopolitan Hotel is only a few steps away, housing a saloon, billiard hall, barbershop, and spotless bathrooms well appointed with toilet soaps, bay rum, and even needles, thread, and buttons.

Two other popular inns stand at the foot of the Four Mile Trail to Glacier Point: Black's Hotel is a long, shed-like hostelry, while Leidig's two-story inn is known for Mrs. Leidig's fine table.

There are myriad excursions to occupy your days. Venture into Tenaya Canyon – always on the lookout for bear, of course – to see Mirror Lake's unrippled waters reflect Mount Watkins. Or strike out for magnificent Vernal Fall by climbing the steep ladder hammered into the rock. Be alert for rattlers there. You'll undoubtedly be drenched by the cascade's mist, but it will never quench your exhilaration. The excursion will be easier if you spend the night at Snow's Casa Nevada, a mountain chalet at the base of the fall. From there, hike on to the Nevada Fall, which slides over a broad parapet of stone before projecting itself downward through space.

Among the accommodations in Yosemite, Leidig's Hotel is known for its food, a nice change from decades past, when meals in the park's inns were haphazard.

And finally, be sure to ride the 4-mile toll path to Glacier Point, where James McCauley has built his Mountain House. Here you can crouch on the granite shelf that juts out over the valley and contemplate a view that stretches to distant Sierra peaks. The evening campfires are an excuse to marvel at the inky dome of stars. McCauley often caps off the evening – and delights the tourists in the valley below – by pushing the dying embers off the cliff in an unforgettable firefall.

Who could turn down such a journey? Go now, before greater hordes crowd the mountain paths where birdsong is still the loudest noise. Already one journalist – a former sawyer and enthusiastic mountaineer named John Muir – is warning of the dangers of losing this wild place. Perhaps someone will heed his words and create a park that truly belongs to the entire nation.

A NEW VOICE FOR YOSEMITE

One man, it seems, can read Yosemite like a book. When John Muir first visited the valley in 1868, he was awestruck by the magnificent natural world he encountered. He returned the next year to work as a shepherd and then ran a sawmill for hotelkeeper James Hutchings. During those two years the young bearded Scot took every opportunity to study Yosemite's mountains, canyons, and waterfalls, mapping and measuring, and keeping copious notes. He lived in a simple, handmade cabin, but famous visitors, including Ralph Waldo Emerson, found their way to his door.

Now Muir has begun to publish articles about Yosemite, and his notion that glaciers, not some violent occurrence, are responsible for the shape of the canyon and its rocky wonders has sent shock waves through the scientific establishment. He's also started a campaign to protect Yosemite's extraordinary wilderness. "I often wonder what men will do with the mountains," he writes. "Will he cut down all, and make ships and houses with the trees? If so, what will be the final and far upshot?"

AUTHOR'S NOTE

The Wild West lasted perhaps twenty-five years after the end of the Civil War, an astonishingly short time, considering the era's impact on popular culture ever since. This guide is set at the end of 1880, when the way of life that has given rise to so many books, television shows, movies, and obsessions was still extant and famous events like the gunfight at O.K. Corral and the death of Jesse James were yet to come. I've tried to keep people, landmarks, and events exactly where they happened to be in 1880, though there is conflicting information – and many competing theories – about almost everything. For quotations I've used only contemporary accounts in books, magazines, memoirs, and diaries, but I have relied on later scholarship – everything from biographies and histories to picture books – to buttress the descriptions.

What I have not faithfully reported are the frequently articulated prejudices of the times. Native Americans, Chinese, Mexicans, Jews, and others were objects of biased, vitriolic preconceptions and too often actual victims as well. I have left out the slurs not to diminish what minorities of all kinds suffered in the late 19th century, but because I'm sure that you – as a time traveler from a supposedly more enlightened age – would also have considered these comments beneath notice.

I'd like to thank Thames & Hudson for having enough confidence in me to ask me to take on this project and shepherding the book with enthusiasm.

The resources at Davidson Library, University of California, Santa Barbara, are phenomenal, and I couldn't have written this book without access to their open stacks, thanks to the Friends of the UCSB Library. I very much appreciate the invitation of the Santa Ynez Valley Historical Museum to attend their 2009 symposium on the stagecoach.

I'd also like to thank Cynthia Brown for her advice and support, as well as William Scheller for his helpful comments about firearms. I'm grateful, too, for the hospitality of Carolyn and Chris Eichin in Virginia City, Nevada; their appreciation for the history of the town was contagious.

And of course I'd like to thank my husband, Steve Siegel, to whom this book is dedicated. He has spent his entire career trying to interest students in history and social studies, and when we had an opportunity, he never hesitated for an instant to "go West."

Joan Tapper

WASHINGTON
TERRITORY

Columbia River

Portland

Willamette River

OREGON

IDAHO
TERRITORY

MONTANA TERRIT

Bozeman   Livingsto

Yellowstone
National Park

Snake River

WYOMI
TERRIT

Central Pacific RR   Ogden

Great
Salt Lake   Salt Lake Cit

Redding

Reno

Virginia City

Sacramento   Carson City

San Francisco

Modesto

Merced

Yosemite
Valley

NEVADA   UTAH TERRITORY

CALIFORNIA

Los
Angeles

Southern Pacific RR

ARIZONA
TERRITORY

Prescott

Phoenix

Yuma

Benson   Tom

THE
WILD WEST
1880

0   300

miles

missouri River

Bismark ● ─────────── ● **Fargo** — *Northern Pacific RR* — **Duluth** ●

DAKOTA TERRITORY

MINNESOTA

WISCONSIN

Minneapolis/St. Paul ●

ighorn
ield

Deadwood ●

h Platte River

Milwaukee ●

IOWA

Chicago ●

Fort Laramie ●

NEBRASKA

Chicago, Milwaukee & St Paul RR

Cheyenne ●

Platte River

Omaha ●

Chicago, Rock Island & Pacific RR

Union Pacific RR

*Denver &
Rio Grande RR*

Chicago, Burlington & RR

Denver ●

MISSOURI

ILLINOIS

Colorado Springs ●

KANSAS

Topeka ●

Kansas City ●

Pueblo ●

Arkansas River

St. Louis ●

RADO

La Junta ● ─── **Dodge City** ●

Missouri Pacific RR

Wichita ●

*Atchison, Topeka
& Santa Fe RR*

INDIAN TERRITORY

Santa Fe
uquerque

Canadian River

ARKANSAS

KENTUCKY

TENNESSEE

MEXICO
ITORY

Red River

*Missouri, Kansas
& Texas RR*

Texas & Pacific RR

MISSISSIPPI

Mississippi River

Paso

Dallas ●

Fort Worth ●

MISSISSIPPI

Marshall ●

LOUISIANA

ALABAMA

TEXAS

Rio Grande

San Antonio ●

San Antonio RR

Galveston ●

New Orleans ●

INDEX

★ 157 ★

★ ★ ★ ★ ★

First published in 2010 in paperback in the United States of America by Thames & Hudson Inc., 500 Fifth Avenue, New York, New York 10110

thamesandhudsonusa.com

Library of Congress Catalog Card Number 2009936859

ISBN 978-0-500-28872-6

Printed and bound in China by Toppan Leefung